EVERYTHING

YOU NEED TO KNOW ABOUT

ARIES

EVERYTHING
YOU NEED TO KNOW ABOUT

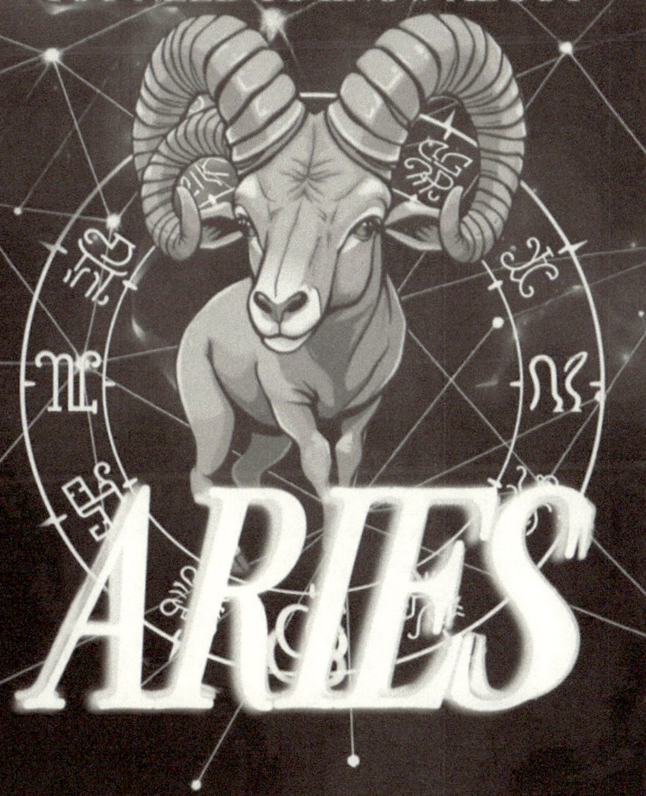

ARIES

Contents

Preface

Welcome to Everything You Need to Know About Aries, a book designed to immerse you in the world of this bold and dynamic zodiac sign. Aries is more than just the first sign of the zodiac—it is a force of energy, passion, and determination. Whether you're an Aries yourself, love someone who is, or simply enjoy the fascinating world of astrology, this book is your ultimate guide to understanding the Ram in all its fiery glory.

Inside these pages, you'll find a deep dive into the Aries personality—what makes them tick, what fuels their ambition, and what ignites their temper. You'll explore the ruling planet of Mars and how it shapes their fearless approach to life. You'll uncover their luckiest charms, numbers, plants, and feng shui elements, all tied to their natural energy. Whether you're curious about Aries' compatibility with other signs or want an in-depth analysis of every Aries birthdate, this book offers something for everyone.

Astrology has been studied and refined for centuries, and this collection draws upon generations of wisdom, chart interpretations, and forecasting to give you the most comprehensive view of Aries possible. Read it for insight, use it for fun, and share it with family and friends as you uncover the strengths, quirks, and complexities of this remarkable zodiac sign.

Enjoy the journey, and may the bold spirit of Aries inspire you along the way!

Chapter One

Aries in Astrology

Aries, the first sign of the zodiac, is known for its dynamic and assertive nature. People born under this sign are often described as confident, independent, and driven individuals. Represented by the symbol of the Ram, Aries embodies a strong-willed and determined personality that thrives on leadership, action, and the pursuit of new challenges.

As a cardinal fire sign, Aries naturally takes the lead, embracing the qualities of initiation and an unstoppable spirit. Their enthusiasm and energy drive them to seize opportunities, and they are rarely content with standing still. Ruled by Mars, the planet of action and aggression, Aries possesses a passionate nature that fuels their courage, competitiveness, and determination. This influence makes them bold in their pursuits, unafraid to go after what they want, and willing to push boundaries to achieve their goals.

Aries individuals are known for their pioneering spirit, always eager to explore uncharted territories and embrace the unknown. They are not ones to shy away from risk, often preferring to forge their own path rather than follow the footsteps of others. This adventurous nature is deeply ingrained in their identity, and they constantly seek new experiences that excite and challenge them.

Independence is a core trait of Aries, as they value their freedom and autonomy above all else. They prefer to rely on themselves rather than depend on others, trusting their instincts and forging ahead with confidence. Their self-reliance allows them to make bold decisions without hesitation, though at times, this can make them resistant to outside influence or advice.

With boundless energy and enthusiasm, Aries is always on the move, constantly seeking excitement and action. They thrive in fast-paced environments that keep them engaged, whether through physical activity, competition, or high-stakes challenges. Their spontaneous nature often leads them to act on impulse, following their instincts rather than overanalyzing situations. While this can result in occasional missteps, Aries embraces every experience as an opportunity for growth and learning.

Their competitive nature drives them to excel in all aspects of life. Whether in sports, career, or personal endeavors, Aries strives to be the best, pushing themselves to outperform others and achieve their ambitions. Recognition and accomplishment fuel their motivation, as they take pride in their successes and the impact they make on the world.

Aries' fiery passion extends to their emotions, making them quick-tempered but also quick to forgive. Their intensity can sometimes lead to conflicts, yet they rarely hold grudges. Their outbursts are often short-lived, and their natural optimism allows them to move forward without dwelling on negativity. Their direct and straightforward communication style reflects their honesty and confidence. They value open dialogue and have little patience for ambiguity or manipulation.

Despite their assertiveness, Aries possesses a generous and protective side, particularly toward their loved ones. Their loyalty is unwavering, and they will go to great lengths to support and defend those they care about. Their protective instincts make them reliable friends and allies, always ready to stand up for what they believe in.

While Aries thrives on challenges, their restless nature can lead to impatience. They crave constant stimulation and may struggle with tasks requiring long-term commitment or repetitive routines. Their short attention span pushes them to seek new adventures, sometimes abandoning projects before completion in favor of something more exciting.

Finding balance is essential for Aries, as their strong-willed nature can sometimes overshadow the perspectives and needs of others. Developing patience and learning to listen can enhance their relationships and overall success. When they channel their boundless energy with mindfulness and purpose, Aries becomes an unstoppable force, leaving a lasting impact wherever they go.

With their fearless determination, pioneering spirit, and unwavering drive, Aries stands as a beacon of passion and leadership. Their journey is one of bold action, constant movement, and a relentless pursuit of greatness, making them one of the most dynamic and inspiring signs of the zodiac.

Chapter Two

Aries and Its Ruling Planet, Mars

Aries is ruled by the dynamic and assertive planet Mars, a connection that plays a significant role in shaping the personality, characteristics, and behaviors of individuals born under this sign. Mars, often called the "Warrior Planet," embodies energy, passion, action, and aggression, qualities that are deeply ingrained in Aries. Just as Mars represents a force ready to charge forward, Aries individuals are natural warriors, always prepared to face challenges head-on and take decisive action without hesitation.

The influence of Mars instills Aries with a strong sense of self and individuality. They possess an independent spirit and an innate ability to take the lead in many aspects of life. Their relentless drive pushes them toward their goals, and they are unafraid to assert themselves, ensuring their presence is noticed. The fiery energy of Mars fuels their enthusiasm and zest for life, making them eager to embrace new experiences and pursue thrilling adventures. Aries are often seen as trailblazers, unafraid to step into the unknown and take risks that others might avoid.

The competitive nature of Aries is another direct effect of Mars' influence. Aries thrives in competitive environments, relishing the thrill of victory and pushing themselves to be the best at whatever they set their sights on. Mars grants them the courage and determination needed to conquer obstacles, reinforcing their relentless pursuit of success. The drive to achieve, to stand out, and to be first is an intrinsic part of Aries' identity, making them formidable competitors in any field they choose.

While Mars gifts Aries with boldness and energy, it also manifests in impulsive and hot-headed tendencies. Aries can be quick to react, acting on instinct before considering the consequences. Their fiery nature may lead them to make rash decisions, speaking or acting before fully thinking things through. Learning to channel this energy constructively is essential for Aries, helping them develop patience and self-control to balance their assertiveness with thoughtful decision-making.

The influence of Mars extends to Aries' physical vitality. Many Aries individuals possess a natural athleticism and strong physical presence, often feeling an innate need for movement and activity. They thrive in environments that allow them to release pent-up energy, whether through sports, exercise, or engaging in physical challenges. This boundless energy gives them remarkable stamina, pushing them to keep going long after others have tired out.

Mars, as a planetary force in astrology, is one of the most powerful and influential celestial bodies. It represents raw energy, action, desire, passion, and assertiveness. Its position in an individual's birth chart provides insight into their ambition, drive, and how they handle conflict. Mars rules over our basic instincts and primal urges, acting as the internal fire that fuels motivation and determination. It governs physical energy and stamina, enabling individuals to actively pursue their goals with unwavering commitment.

The way a person expresses their desires and asserts themselves is often influenced by Mars' placement in their chart. It dictates their approach to competition, their ability to stand up for themselves, and their willingness to take risks. Mars also governs sexual energy and attraction, shaping the way people pursue and experience intimate connections. The passion, sensuality, and intensity associated with Mars can drive Aries to seek deep and meaningful experiences in their relationships.

Beyond personal traits, Mars influences external events and circumstances. It is linked to conflict, aggression, and power struggles, often serving as a catalyst for change. Aries, under Mars' influence, are not afraid to confront challenges head-on, standing firm in their beliefs and fighting for what they think is right. This bold and fearless nature allows them to navigate life with a warrior's mindset, facing adversity with determination and resilience.

The way Mars' energy manifests in an individual's life depends on its position in their birth chart and its interactions with other planets. When Mars forms harmonious aspects with other planets, it can result in a healthy expression of drive, motivation, and ambition, leading to success and vitality. Challenging aspects, on the other hand, may contribute to impulsive behavior, anger issues, or conflicts that require resolution. For Aries, understanding and harnessing Mars' influence can help them refine their strengths and channel their energy in a way that fosters growth, achievement, and personal fulfillment.

With Mars as their ruling planet, Aries embody the essence of action, courage, and determination. They are pioneers, competitors, and fearless adventurers who thrive on challenges and the pursuit of their ambitions. Their fiery passion, combined with the relentless energy of Mars, ensures that Aries individuals leave a lasting impact on the world around them, driven by an unyielding spirit that refuses to back down.

Chapter Three

Aries and the Element Fire

Aries share an intimate bond with the element of fire, which serves as a symbol of their passionate and dynamic nature. Fire acts as the driving force behind their actions, motivations, and overall personalities, embodying the primal energy that propels them forward and sets them ablaze with an unwavering determination.

Like the nature of fire itself, Aries exude warmth, enthusiasm, and vitality, captivating others with their fiery spirit. Their souls are ignited by the flames of fire, empowering them to confront challenges head-on and wholeheartedly embrace the boundless opportunities life presents. These trailblazers constantly seek new adventures, pushing the limits of what is deemed possible.

Creativity and inspiration are intrinsically tied to fire, and Aries skillfully harness this element to fuel their artistic endeavors. Just as fire consumes fuel to generate heat and light, Aries channel their inner fire to produce art, music, writing, and various forms of creative expression. They are driven by a profound desire to awaken the passion within themselves and others, aiming to leave a lasting impact through their artistic creations.

However, akin to the dual nature of fire, Aries possess both comforting and destructive aspects. They are warm and charismatic, capable of bringing joy and inspiration to those around them. Nevertheless, their fiery temperament can sometimes lead to impulsive actions and fiery outbursts when their boundaries are crossed. Thus, Aries must learn to harness the transformative power of fire, utilizing it as a tool for personal growth and positive change.

Fire stands as a symbol of transformation and renewal, embodying the very essence of Aries lives. They possess an innate ability to rise from the ashes of adversity, reinventing themselves with resilience. In the face of challenges, Aries find the strength to conquer obstacles, emerging stronger and more resilient than before. Fire fuels their drive for self-improvement, enabling them to embrace change with open arms and embark on a journey of personal evolution.

Natural leaders, Aries embody the qualities associated with fire. They possess an inherent ability to inspire and motivate others, leading them towards their aspirations with passion and charisma. Just as fire spreads and influences its surroundings, Aries leave a profound impact on the people they encounter. Their fiery spirit and unwavering determination ignite a spark within others, empowering them to act and pursue their dreams.

Chapter Four

Layers of Aries: Beyond the Zodiac Sun Sign

While the sun sign provides a glimpse into the core essence of an individual, investigating the intricacies of Aries' moon sign, rising sign, and other astrological placements unveils a richer tapestry of their personality. Each element in the astrological chart contributes its unique hue to the portrait of an Aries, adding nuance, depth, and complexity to their cosmic blueprint.

Aries' Moon Sign

The moon sign reflects one's emotional landscape and inner world. For an Aries, the moon sign adds a layer of emotional intelligence and receptivity. If the moon is in a sign like Cancer, Aries may display heightened sensitivity and nurturing tendencies, while a moon in Sagittarius could bring an adventurous and optimistic flavor to their emotional responses.

Aries' Rising Sign (Ascendant)

The rising sign, or ascendant, sets the stage for how others perceive an Aries upon first meeting. An Aries with a Gemini rising, for example, may exhibit communicative and witty qualities, while a Taurus rising could lend an air of determination and steadfastness.

Influence of Mars

As the ruling planet of Aries, Mars plays a pivotal role in shaping their drive, ambition, and assertiveness. The sign Mars occupies in the birth chart provides insights into how Aries assert themselves and pursue their goals.

Mercury Placement

Mercury, the planet of communication, influences how Aries express themselves intellectually. An Aries with Mercury in Aries may bring directness and a quick-witted approach to their communication style, while Mercury in Leo emphasizes their natural confidence and expressive abilities.

Venus Placement

While not traditionally associated with Aries, Venus still influences their love style and aesthetic preferences. The sign Venus occupies in the birth chart provides insights into how Aries approach relationships and what they find personally fulfilling.

Influence of the 1st House

The 1st house in the birth chart is associated with the self and personal identity. The sign occupying this house and any planets within it shed light on how Aries navigate their individuality, self-image, and approach to life.

Nuances in the Natal Chart

Examining the overall placement of planets in different houses of the natal chart provides nuanced insights into various aspects of an Aries' life. For instance, a concentration of planets in the 9th house may signify a strong focus on exploration, philosophy, and intellectual pursuits.

How These Placements Add Nuance

Depth to Emotional Expression: The moon sign reveals how Aries process and express their emotions, adding depth and complexity to their interpersonal relationships. It influences their intuitive responses and what they need for emotional fulfillment.

Persona and First Impressions: The rising sign shapes the outward persona and initial impressions that Aries make on others. It influences their style, approachability, and the way they project themselves into the world.

Communication Styles: Mercury's placement affects how Aries articulate thoughts and ideas. It adds layers to their communication style, whether it's marked by passion, analytical precision, or directness.

Motivations and Actions: Mars' influence guides Aries in how they pursue their desires and objectives. It provides insights into their driving force, assertiveness, and approach to challenges.

Relationship Dynamics: While Venus is not traditionally associated with Aries, its placement offers a nuanced understanding of their approach to relationships, including their values, expectations, and the qualities they seek in a partner.

Life Themes and Focus Areas: The overall configuration of the natal chart sheds light on key life themes and areas of focus for Aries. It provides a comprehensive view of their strengths, challenges, and potential areas of growth.

By unraveling the layers of Aries' astrological chart, one can appreciate the multidimensional nature of their personality. Astrology beyond the sun sign serves as a cosmic compass, guiding Aries through the intricacies of their individual journey and highlighting the diverse facets that contribute to their celestial identity.

Chapter Five

Aries in Retrograde

Retrograde periods, marked by the apparent backward motion of planets in their orbits, bring a distinctive cosmic energy to the experiences of Aries. As trailblazers and warriors of the zodiac, Aries may face unique challenges during these celestial reversals, but they also present valuable opportunities for self-discovery and personal evolution. This exploration delves into how Aries may navigate retrograde periods, offering insights into their influences and strategies for mastering the cosmic backtrack.

Mars, the ruling planet of Aries, occasionally enters retrograde motion, impacting their dynamic and assertive nature. During Mars retrograde, Aries may find their usual drive and boldness tempered. This period prompts a reassessment of goals, desires, and the assertive energy they bring to their endeavors.

Aries, known for their direct and assertive communication style, may encounter challenges during Mercury retrograde. Communication breakdowns, delays, or misunderstandings can disrupt their naturally straightforward dialogue. Patience and clarity become paramount as Aries faces these hurdles.

Retrogrades, particularly involving Mars, encourage Aries to consider self-reflection on their independence and self-identity. They may find themselves questioning their autonomy, reevaluating their goals, and seeking clarity on what true personal freedom means to them.

Strategies for Retrograde Challenges: a. **Patience and Flexibility**

Aries can navigate retrograde challenges by cultivating patience and flexibility. Acknowledging that setbacks are temporary and embracing adaptability can alleviate the frustration that may arise.

- Retrogrades provide an ideal time for Aries to engage in personal introspection. Practices like journaling, meditation, or self-assessment can offer valuable insights into their goals, desires, and the alignment of their actions with their authentic selves.

- During Mercury retrograde, maintaining clear and direct communication becomes crucial. Aries can overcome communication challenges by expressing themselves with precision, avoiding assumptions, and confirming details to avoid misunderstandings.

- Aries may use retrogrades as periods for reassessing their personal goals. They can reflect on whether their aspirations align with their authentic desires and whether adjustments are needed for a more fulfilling and harmonious life.

- Mars retrograde might trigger self-doubt or frustration in Aries. Cultivating self-validation and recognizing personal achievements can counteract these feelings, fostering a resilient sense of self-worth.

- Retrogrades can introduce uncertainty, requiring Aries to make strategic decisions. Engaging in thoughtful decision-making, seeking advice from trusted allies, and considering the potential consequences contribute to balanced choices.

Embracing Evolutionary Opportunities

Rather than viewing retrogrades solely as obstacles, Aries can embrace them as opportunities for personal and professional evolution. These celestial shifts encourage self-awareness, fostering a deeper understanding of personal desires, assertive tendencies, and the dynamics of their individual journey.

Aries may find strength in seeking support from their community, friends, or partners during retrograde periods. Open discussions, shared concerns, and collaborative problem-solving can help them navigate challenges with a sense of unity.

As Aries encounters retrograde periods, they can perceive these cosmic events not as hindrances but as cosmic mentors guiding them toward deeper self-discovery and refined assertiveness. By embodying patience, adaptability, and introspective practices, Aries can boldly navigate the retrograde journey, emerging with newfound insights and a reinforced commitment to their unique path in the cosmic dance.

Chapter Six

Positive Traits of Aries

Aries, the first sign of the zodiac, is associated with dynamic and assertive qualities. Persons born under the sign of Aries often exhibit a range of positive attributes that contribute to their vibrant and go-getter personality.

- Aries men and women are known for their fearless approach to life. They tackle challenges head-on, showing remarkable courage in the face of adversity. This fearlessness allows them to take risks and embrace new opportunities with enthusiasm.

- High energy levels are a hallmark of Aries. They exude vitality and enthusiasm, infusing their surroundings with a contagious dynamism. This energy often propels them to initiate projects, inspire others, and lead by example.

• Aries own strong leadership qualities. Their assertiveness and confidence naturally place them in leadership roles. They thrive in situations where they can take charge, make decisions, and motivate others to follow their lead.

• Positivity is a key trait of Aries. They maintain an optimistic outlook even in challenging situations. This positive mindset helps them overcome obstacles, inspiring those around them to adopt a can-do attitude.

• Aries have a natural inclination for adventure. They embrace the spirit of exploration, seeking out new experiences and challenges. This pioneering attitude often leads them to discover innovative solutions and break new ground.

• Independence is highly valued by Aries and it goes without saying that they prefer to carve their own path and make decisions autonomously. This independent mindset fosters self-reliance and a sense of autonomy in their personal and professional pursuits.

- Whether pursuing personal goals, professional endeavors, or relationships, Aries persons invest themselves wholeheartedly. This passion contributes to their drive, determination, and a willingness to overcome obstacles.

- Aries is the initiator of the zodiac, and individuals born under this sign are natural trailblazers. They are not afraid to take the lead, initiate projects, and explore uncharted territories. Their pioneering spirit often sparks inspiration in others.

- Aries are direct and are known for their straightforward and honest communication style. They value clarity and prefer to express their thoughts openly. This directness contributes to effective communication and prevents misunderstandings.

- Resilience is a strength of Aries. When faced with setbacks or challenges, they display tenacity and determination to bounce back. Their ability to persevere in the pursuit of their goals is a testament to their resilient nature.

- Aries have a generous and protective nature, especially towards their loved ones. They are willing to go to great lengths to support and defend those they care about, demonstrating a strong sense of loyalty.

- Aries bring spontaneity and a sense of adventure to their interactions. Their fun-loving nature makes them enjoyable companions, and they often infuse excitement into social gatherings with their spirited presence.

Aries are a bag full of positive attributes that make them formidable leaders, inspiring companions, and resilient individuals in the pursuit of their goals. Their dynamic and courageous spirit contributes to their ability to navigate life's challenges with enthusiasm and optimism.

Chapter Seven

Aries Negative Traits

Aries like everyone else, can exhibit negative traits. It's important to note that these traits may not be universally applicable to all Aries, as personality varies widely among people. Here are some potential negative traits associated with Aries:

- It is well documented that Aries can be impulsive, often acting without thoroughly considering the consequences. This impulsiveness can lead to hasty decisions that may not be well thought out.

- Aries can be highly impatient, wanting immediate results and gratification. This impatience may make it challenging for them to endure long processes or wait for things to unfold naturally.

- Unfortunately, Aries, although passionate and fiery in nature, can sometimes be short tempered. They may get angry quickly and find it challenging to control their emotions.

- While healthy competition can be motivating, Aries may take it to an extreme, making them overly competitive. This competitiveness can strain relationships, especially if winning becomes more important than collaboration.

- Aries can be stubborn and resistant to changing their opinions or adapting to different viewpoints. This inflexibility may hinder their ability to compromise in certain situations.

- Driven by their assertive nature, Aries often appear self-centered. Their focus on personal goals and desires might overshadow the needs and perspectives of others. No, they are not egomaniacs, just, at times, self-absorbed.

- Aries enjoy taking risks, but this trait can become a negative when it leads to reckless behavior. They might be prone to taking unnecessary risks without considering the potential consequences.

- This group of men and women are big-picture thinkers, but they may overlook details in their enthusiasm to move forward. This oversight can lead to mistakes or oversights in tasks that require careful attention.

Chapter Eight

An Aries Woman

A woman born under the zodiac sign of Aries is known for her unique qualities. Here is a list of these characteristics:

- An Aries woman is naturally passionate and ready to face life's challenges. She is full of energy and desires to achieve her dreams and goals. Her creative thinking and ability to create allow her to excel in the fields of art, music, and other forms of expression.

- She has a strong persona, self-confidence, has firm convictions and is certain of her own identity. She is often recognized for her ability to speak her mind freely, even in the face of opposition. Her willingness to express her opinions gives her the power to lead and take charge.

- An Aries woman possesses a courageous spirit and is

ready to confront life's challenges with bravery. She can persevere despite obstacles and setbacks. Her determination and persistence empower her to fight for and defend her dreams.

- Despite her bold outward personality, an Aries woman has a tender heart and is ready to give love. When she falls in true love, she becomes sensual, affectionate, and emotional. Her love creates a beautiful and fragrant environment where her romantic qualities flourish.

- An Aries woman is naturally full of enthusiasm and joy. She is ready to embark on new adventures and freely explore things that are new and different. Her energy and positive outlook on life are contagious, which is why she is often surrounded by people who value her energy and optimistic perspective.

- As a natural leader, an Aries woman can lead and enlighten others. She possesses deep understanding and broad general knowledge that she uses to guide her friends and colleagues towards success. Her ability to inspire and offer advice allows her to be a teacher and mentor to her friends.

- An Aries woman often forms wide and diverse circles of friends. This is because of her ever-changing interests, and not everyone she encounters can keep up with all her desires. However, this is not a problem for her as she has enough self-confidence to approach different people and make friends. Despite having many friends, she selectively chooses a few to be close to her.

These qualities of an Aries woman allow her to be a unique individual full of energy, courage, and love. She is an intelligent leader, a loving partner, and a devoted friend who continues to inspire those around her.

Chapter Nine

An Aries Man

An Aries man possesses a multitude of unique qualities that make him stand out. Enjoy a rather expansive description of these characteristics:

- The Aries man is always proud of himself. He has unwavering confidence that cannot be easily shaken by any zodiac sign. He is certain of his own identity and embraces his individuality. This self-assurance gives him a strong presence and an air of authority.

- The Aries man can be an assertive and sometimes even aggressive individual. However, he knows when to channel his assertiveness and control his temper. He understands the importance of managing his emotions and uses his assertiveness constructively to achieve his goals.

- When it comes to love, an Aries man is the one who makes his own decisions. He is not afraid to express his feelings or do immediately what needs to be done. He values his own judgment and holds the power to make decisions for himself. He is a focused and determined individual, even when it comes to matters of the heart.

- An Aries man is driven by passion and always seeks excitement in life. He has a thirst for adventure and loves to take on new challenges. Whether it's exploring unfamiliar places, trying new activities, or taking risks, he thrives on the thrill of the unknown. His passion fuels his drive and inspires those around him.

- While the Aries man can be strong-willed, he also values respect and consideration in his relationships. If his partner exhibits a strong personality and stands her ground, he respects her as an equal in the bedroom. He does not intend to harm or manipulate, but rather seeks mutual respect and fulfillment in a sexual relationship.

- The Aries man is ambitious by nature and possesses a creative mindset. He aims high and sets ambitious goals for himself. He is not afraid to take the lead and assumes responsibility for his work. However, he also needs to learn to trust and delegate to others to achieve his desired outcomes effectively.

- The Aries man is often considered the life of the party. His charisma and magnetic personality draw people towards him. He can inspire and motivate others, leading them in a positive direction. His leadership qualities make him a natural influencer and a source of inspiration for his friends and acquaintances.

- Once an Aries man forms a deep connection, he is fiercely loyal and supportive. He stands by his loved ones through thick and thin, providing unwavering support. His loyalty extends to his friendships as well, where he values true and lasting connections with a select few.

These qualities of an Aries man make him a dynamic and captivating individual. He exudes confidence, assertiveness, and independence, while also possessing a passionate and adventurous spirit. With his ambition, creativity, and natural charisma, he inspires and influences those around him.

Chapter Ten

Lucky Stars: Aries Fortunate Moments

In astrology, luck is believed to be influenced by a range of factors, including the positioning of celestial bodies and their interactions with an individual's birth chart. While luck can be subjective and can vary for each person, here are some periods when Aries may be considered more likely to experience positive outcomes:

The period when the Sun is in Aries, typically from March 21 to April 19, is considered an energetically charged time for Aries. This period aligns with their natural attributes and can amplify their luck, confidence, and vitality.

Remember that Mars is the ruling planet of Aries, and its transits can have a significant impact on Aries luck. Therefore, when Mars aligns favorably with other planets or makes harmonious aspects in their birth chart, it can enhance their energy, motivation, and assertiveness, increasing their chances of success and favorable outcomes.

Jupiter Transits

Jupiter, the planet associated with luck and expansion, can bring opportunities and blessings when it transits through beneficial positions in an Aries birth chart. Jupiter's favorable aspects or its presence in Aries or other compatible signs can signify a period of growth, abundance, and fortunate circumstances.

New Moon in Aries

The New Moon in Aries, which occurs annually in late March or early April, is a potent time for setting intentions and initiating new projects. Aries may find this period particularly auspicious for launching endeavors, making important decisions, or embarking on personal growth journeys.

Personal Planetary Alignments

Each Aries has a unique birth chart with specific planetary positions. Analyzing the aspects and transits of their ruling planet Mars, as well as other significant planets like Venus, Jupiter, and the Moon, can provide insights into periods of increased luck and positive influences in their lives.

Aries and Career

Aries are known for their ambitious and determined nature when it comes to their careers. They possess a relentless drive and an unwavering commitment to success, which propels them to excel in their chosen fields.

With their natural leadership abilities and confidence, Aries thrive in positions of authority and are often drawn to careers that allow them to take charge and make independent decisions. They are not afraid to assert themselves in the professional realm. Aries have a remarkable ability to inspire and motivate others, making them effective leaders and influencers.

Aries have a competitive spirit and enjoy challenges. They thrive in fast-paced environments where they can prove their skills and rise to the top. Their assertiveness and drive for achievement enable them to pursue ambitious goals and surpass expectations. Aries are not easily deterred by setbacks and obstacles. Instead, they view challenges as opportunities for growth and innovation.

In the workplace, Aries are known for their exceptional work ethic and dedication. They are not afraid to put in the necessary effort and go the extra mile to accomplish their objectives. Aries have a great deal of energy and enthusiasm, which allows them to tackle demanding tasks with vigor and determination. They are often admired for their ability to handle pressure and maintain a positive attitude in stressful situations.

Aries have a natural affinity for entrepreneurship and enjoy being their own boss. They strive for independence and autonomy in their careers, and they thrive in environments where they can take control of their professional destiny. Aries are not afraid to take risks and venture into new territories. They possess a pioneering spirit and are often at the forefront of innovation and change.

However, they should be mindful of their impulsive nature and tendency to jump into new ventures without careful planning. It is important for them to balance their enthusiasm with a strategic approach to ensure long-term success. Aries can benefit from surrounding themselves with trusted advisors who can provide guidance and help them channel their energy effectively.

Aries excel in careers that allow them to be creative. They enjoy being at the forefront of new projects and taking the lead in implementing innovative ideas. They are adept at identifying opportunities for growth and advancement.

In the workplace, Aries value honesty, integrity, and direct communication. They appreciate colleagues and superiors who are straightforward and transparent. Aries are not afraid to express their opinions and voice their ideas, making them valuable contributors to team projects and discussions.

Aries bring a dynamic and enterprising spirit to their careers. They own the drive, confidence, and determination to succeed in their chosen paths. Their natural leadership abilities, competitive nature, and innovative mindset set them apart in the professional realm. With their ambitious and relentless pursuit of success, Aries make a significant impact in their careers and strive to leave a legacy.

Chapter Twelve

Aries and Family

Aries are renowned for their self-reliant and self-assured disposition, which permeates their approach to family life. They infuse their dynamic vitality and fervor into their roles as parents, siblings, and children, fostering a spirited and vivacious family atmosphere.

As parents, Aries have a natural assertiveness and assume leadership with ease. They possess a deep-seated desire to guide and mentor their children, instilling in them self-assurance and autonomy. Aries parents are fiercely protective, going to great lengths to ensure their children's happiness and well-being. They wholeheartedly encourage their children to pursue their passions and offer unwavering support in their endeavors.

Authenticity and honesty are highly esteemed by Aries in their familial connections. Their communication style is forthright and unambiguous, occasionally perceived as assertive or even confrontational. Nevertheless, their aim is to foster an environment of open and candid dialogue within the family. They hold immense value in family members who can match their level of communication and engage in thought-provoking conversations.

A strong need for individuality can occasionally lead to clashes within family dynamics. They hold their independence and freedom in high regard, and they expect the same for their family members. Aries actively encourage their loved ones to express their unique selves and pursue their personal aspirations. However, they also harbor grand expectations and may push their family members to strive for excellence and attain greatness.

With a natural inclination for leadership, Aries often assume the role of decision-makers within the family unit. Fearlessly taking charge, they make significant choices that promote the well-being of the family. While their assertiveness proves advantageous in certain situations, Aries must strike a balance by considering the input and needs of other family members.

Renowned for their boundless energy and enthusiasm, Aries infuse family life with an aura of excitement and adventure. They relish in planning and engaging in enjoyable activities that create enduring memories for their loved ones. Arie are natural initiators and frequently take the lead in organizing family outings, vacations, and gatherings.

Nevertheless, Aries should remain mindful of their impulsive nature. At times, they may act without fully contemplating the consequences or hastily make decisions that impact the entire family. Cultivating patience and practicing self-control are imperative for them to ensure their actions align with the long-term well-being of the family.

All in all, Aries bring their vibrant and energetic nature into their familial relationships. They highly value honesty, independence, and authenticity within the family unit. While their assertiveness and strong leadership qualities infuse direction and excitement, Aries must strike a harmonious balance between their individuality and the needs and perspectives of their family members. By fostering open communication, mutual respect, and a sense of adventure, Aries can create a dynamic and affectionate family environment.

Chapter Thirteen

Aries and Relationships

Aries bring their passionate and dynamic energy into their love and romantic relationships. They approach love with enthusiasm and a desire for excitement, making them bold and adventurous partners. Here are ten Aries traits that affect their love and romance.

1.Romantic Pursuit

Aries love the thrill of the chase. They enjoy the excitement of pursuing someone they are interested in and are not afraid to make their intentions clear. Aries are direct in expressing their romantic interest, and they appreciate partners who respond with equal enthusiasm and openness.

2.Independent and Assertive

Aries value their independence and individuality, even in romantic relationships. They seek partners who understand and respect their need for personal freedom and autonomy. Aries individuals appreciate a partner who can match their assertiveness and keep up with their dynamic energy.

3.Adventure and Excitement

Aries thrive on excitement and variety in their romantic relationships. They enjoy trying new things, going on spontaneous adventures, and keeping the spark alive. Routine and monotony can be challenging for Aries, so they constantly seek ways to inject passion and spontaneity into their love lives.

4.Honesty and Direct Communication

Aries have a direct and straightforward communication style, which extends to their romantic relationships. They value honesty and authenticity and expect the same from their partners. Aries appreciate partners who can engage in open and transparent communication, sharing their thoughts, desires, and feelings without reservation.

5.Protective and Loyal

Aries are fiercely protective of their loved ones. They are willing to go to great lengths to ensure the happiness and well-being of their partners. Aries are loyal and devoted partners who will stand by their loved ones through thick and thin.

6.Emotional Rollercoaster

Aries can experience intense emotions and mood swings in their romantic relationships. They may go from extreme highs to lows and back again. It's important for Aries to develop emotional awareness and regulation to maintain balance and harmony in their relationships.

7.Need for Freedom

Aries value their independence and personal freedom. They require a partner who understands and respects their need for space and autonomy. Giving Aries room to pursue their individual interests and maintain their independence is essential for a healthy and fulfilling romantic relationship.

8.Communication and Mutual Understanding

Clear and open communication is vital in Aries' romantic relationships. Aries appreciate partners who can engage in stimulating conversations and share their ideas and opinions. They want their partners to be direct and honest in expressing their needs and desires as well.

9.Intimacy and Connection

While Aries may project a strong and independent image, they also crave deep emotional connection and intimacy with their partners. They seek a partner who can understand their innermost desires and connect with them on a profound level.

10.Passionate and Intense

Aries are known for their intense passion and fiery nature when it comes to love. They throw themselves wholeheartedly into their relationships, seeking deep emotional connections and intense experiences. Aries love passionately and express their affection with great fervor.

Aries bring passion, enthusiasm, and a zest for life into their romantic relationships. They value honesty, independence, and adventure. While they can be impulsive and assertive, they also have a deep capacity for love and loyalty. With open communication, mutual respect, and a shared sense of adventure, Aries can create vibrant and fulfilling romantic connections that are filled with excitement and passion.

Chapter Fourteen

Aries Lucky Numbers

In astrology, certain numbers are believed to be lucky for each zodiac sign, including Aries. These numbers are associated with the energy and characteristics of Aries and are believed to bring them good fortune and positive outcomes. Here are the lucky numbers for Aries:

Number 9

The number 9 is considered highly auspicious for Aries. It symbolizes leadership, ambition, and a pioneering spirit, which resonate with the Aries' personality traits. Number 9 is associated with success, creativity, and spiritual growth. Aries may find that this number brings them opportunities for personal and professional advancement.

Number 6

The number 6 is another lucky number for Aries. It represents harmony, balance, and nurturance. Aries can benefit from the energy of this number as it promotes positive relationships, family bonds, and a sense of responsibility. Number 6 is also associated with abundance and material well-being, making it favorable for Aries in financial matters.

Number 1

As the first sign of the zodiac, Aries is associated with the number 1. This number represents individuality, independence, and self-confidence. Aries are often natural-born leaders, and the number 1 reinforces their assertive and courageous nature. Number 1 is considered lucky for Aries as it signifies new beginnings, opportunities, and the ability to manifest their desires. In other words, to make their dreams come true.

Number 8

The number 8 is associated with power, success, and abundance. It represents material and financial prosperity, which can be beneficial for ambitious Aries. Number 8 is believed to attract opportunities for growth and achievement, especially in business and career endeavors. Aries may find that this number brings them luck in financial matters and helps them overcome challenges.

Number 5

The number 5 is associated with adventure, freedom, and versatility. As we have previously discussed, Aries thrive on excitement and variety, and the number 5 aligns with their energetic and spontaneous nature. This number is believed to bring opportunities for travel, exploration, and personal growth. Aries may find that number 5 brings them luck in discovering new experiences and expanding their horizons.

Chapter Fifteen

Aries Lucky Colors

Aries, the first sign of the zodiac, is associated with dynamic and fiery energies. The lucky colors for Aries resonate with their bold and enthusiastic nature, thus reflecting the vibrant spirit that defines this astrological sign.

Red:

Symbolism: Red is the primary and most powerful lucky color for Aries. It represents the ruling planet Mars, which is the planet of energy, action, and assertiveness. Red symbolizes passion, courage, and the boldness that characterizes Aries individuals. It is a color that ignites enthusiasm and propels Aries to take on challenges with vigor.

White:

Symbolism: White is associated with purity and clarity. For Aries, it signifies the clarity of thought and purpose. It complements the intense nature of Aries by bringing a sense of balance and tranquility. White is also linked to new beginnings, aligning with Aries' role as the initiator of the zodiac.

Yellow:

Symbolism: Yellow is a color that represents energy, positivity, and optimism. It resonates with the lively and adventurous spirit of Aries. Yellow is believed to enhance mental clarity and boost creativity, aligning with Aries' dynamic approach to life. It symbolizes the sunshine that Aries brings into any situation.

Orange:

Symbolism: Orange is a vibrant and energetic color that reflects Aries' zest for life. It combines the passion of red with the joyfulness of yellow, creating a dynamic and uplifting energy. Orange is associated with enthusiasm, creativity, and the adventurous nature of Aries individuals.

Gold:

Symbolism: Gold is a color associated with success, abundance, and achievement. It complements Aries' ambitious and goal-oriented personality. Gold represents the rewards that come from Aries' determined efforts and symbolizes the regal nature of this dynamic sign.

Scarlet:

Symbolism: Scarlet, a deep shade of red, resonates with Aries' vigor and determination. It symbolizes strength, courage, and passion. Scarlet is a color that empowers Aries to overcome challenges and stand out with confidence in their pursuits.

Purple:

Symbolism: Purple is linked to mystery, spirituality, and inspiration. For Aries, it represents the depth of their thoughts and the quest for knowledge. Purple is a color that encourages Aries to explore new horizons intellectually while maintaining a sense of mystery and allure.

Turquoise:

Symbolism: Turquoise is a color associated with balance, wisdom, and positive energy. It aligns with Aries' need for equilibrium and fairness. Turquoise encourages Aries to approach situations with a calm and collected demeanor, fostering harmony in their interactions.

Coral:

Symbolism: Coral, a blend of orange and pink, represents a harmonious balance between passion and love. It embodies the social and affectionate side of Aries. Coral is a color that promotes positive relationships and connections, reflecting the sociable nature of Aries individuals.

Silver:

Symbolism: Silver is a color associated with intuition, reflection, and adaptability. It complements Aries' dynamic nature by adding a touch of intuition and adaptability to their approach. Silver symbolizes the versatility and resourcefulness that Aries brings to various situations.

Aries individuals can incorporate these lucky colors into their wardrobes, surroundings, and even in decision-making to enhance their energies and align with the positive attributes of their astrological sign. Whether it's the fiery red or the calming white, these colors resonate with the dynamic and multifaceted nature of Aries, so next time you're shopping, read this chapter before buying anything.

Chapter Sixteen

Aries Lucky Charms

Aries is known for its dynamic and energetic nature. Lucky charms play a fascinating role in channeling and enhancing the positive energies that define the Aries personality. These symbols and talismans resonate with the powerful spirit of Aries, bringing luck, protection, and success.

Ram Symbol:

Representation: The ram is the symbol of Aries, embodying strength, determination, and leadership.

Energies in Aries Favor: Aries can channel the assertive and ambitious energies of the ram as a lucky charm. Ram-themed jewelry, art, or figurines can serve as reminders of their innate power and resilience.

Red Coral:

Representation: Red coral is associated with the planet Mars, the ruling planet of Aries. It symbolizes vitality, passion, and courage.

Energies in Aries Favor: Aries can wear red coral jewelry to enhance their energy levels, boost confidence, and attract positive vibes. It is believed to bring protection and success, aligning with Aries' go-getter attitude.

Diamond:

Representation: Diamonds are gems associated with clarity, strength, and invincibility.

Energies in Aries Favor: Aries can consider diamonds as a lucky charm to enhance mental clarity, promote fearlessness, and attract success. It symbolizes the unyielding spirit of Aries, reflecting their ability to shine brightly in any situation.

Aries Birthstone - Bloodstone:

Representation: Bloodstone is the traditional birthstone for Aries, known for its protective and energizing properties.

Energies in Aries Favor: Aries individuals can wear bloodstone as a charm to boost vitality, courage, and inner strength. It is believed to bring luck, especially during challenging times, reinforcing Aries' resilience.

Mars Talisman:

Representation: A talisman engraved with Mars symbols or sigils.

Energies in Aries Favor: A Mars talisman can serve as a powerful lucky charm for Aries, enhancing their assertiveness, passion, and competitive spirit. It aligns with Aries' connection to the planet of action and energy.

Key Symbol:

Representation: A key, symbolizing unlocking opportunities and success.

Energies in Aries Favor: A key can be a symbolic charm for Aries, representing their ability to unlock doors to new opportunities, achievements, and personal growth. It serves as a reminder of their proactive nature.

Fire Element Symbol:

Representation: Symbols associated with the fire element, such as flames or a candle.

Energies in Aries Favor: Aries, a fire sign, can use fire element symbols as lucky charms to amplify their passionate and dynamic energies. It represents their inner fire, resilience, and the ability to overcome challenges.

Aries Constellation Jewelry:

Representation: Jewelry featuring the constellation of Aries.

Energies in Aries Favor: Aries individuals can wear jewelry depicting their constellation to connect with the cosmic energies that influence their sign. It serves as a personal and celestial talisman, aligning with their astrological identity.

Four-Leaf Clover:

Representation: A rare four-leaf clover.

Energies in Aries Favor: While not traditionally associated with Aries, a four-leaf clover can symbolize luck and good fortune. Aries individuals can embrace it as a charming token for attracting positive outcomes and serendipitous moments.

Sun Symbol:

Representation: The symbol of the sun.

Energies in Aries Favor: Aries, ruled by Mars, can consider the sun symbol as a lucky charm. It represents vitality, energy, and the life force. A sun symbol can enhance Aries' positive energies and vibrant personality.

Aries can choose lucky charms based on personal preferences and resonate with the energies that align with their goals and aspirations. Whether it's the fierce symbol of the ram or the brilliance of diamonds, these charms can serve as powerful reminders of the innate strengths and positive energies that define Aries.

Chapter Seventeen

Aries and Friendships

Aries bring their dynamic and energetic personalities into the realm of friendship, making them vibrant and exciting companions. Governed by Mars, the planet of action and drive, Aries individuals approach friendships with enthusiasm, loyalty, and a zest for exploration. The following lists twelve amazing attributes of being a friend with Aries:

1.Aries is known as the initiator of the zodiac. In friendships, they take the lead in initiating plans, outings, and activities. Their enthusiasm is infectious, making them natural leaders in group dynamics.

2. Aries values loyalty and devotion in friendships. Once they form a connection, they are fiercely protective and stand by their

friends through thick and thin. Aries is the friend who will have your back in any situation.

3. Aries brings an element of spontaneity and adventure to friendships. They thrive on excitement and are always up for trying new things. Whether it's a last-minute road trip or an impromptu gathering, Aries adds a spark of energy.

4. Aries individuals are known for their direct and straight-forward communication. In friendships, they appreciate honesty and expect the same in return. They value friends who communicate openly and don't shy away from expressing their thoughts.

5. Aries friends inject a burst of energy into any social setting. Their dynamic presence is magnetic, and they can easily uplift the mood of the group. Their vitality makes them enjoyable companions for social events.

6. Aries values independence, both in themselves and in their friends. They appreciate friends who have their own pursuits and passions. While Aries is loyal, they also encourage their friends to pursue individual growth.

7. Aries doesn't hold onto grudges for long. In friendships, they are quick to forgive and move on from disagreements.

Their ability to let go of conflicts contributes to the longevity of their friendships.

8. Aries enjoys a friendly competition among friends. Whether it's sports, games, or personal achievements, they see healthy competition as a way to motivate and inspire each other.

9. Aries friends are supportive allies in the pursuit of goals. They encourage their friends to chase their dreams and provide motivational energy. Aries is the friend who believes in your potential and cheers you on.

10. Despite their bold exterior, Aries can be surprisingly thoughtful. They remember important dates, celebrate achievements, and express generosity in their friendships. Aries friends make an effort to show they care.

11. Aries' impulsive nature can lead to challenges in patience, so as a friend or as Aries, this is something to look out for. They might prefer swift decisions and actions, which can be both a strength and a potential source of tension in friendships. Learning to balance their need for speed with the pace of others is a growth area.

12. Aries often takes on a leadership role within friend groups. Their ability to rally others and take charge in organizing events or activities contributes to the cohesion of the group.

In essence, being friends with an Aries means embarking on an exciting journey filled with adventure, loyalty, and a genuine passion for shared experiences. Their dynamic presence and unwavering support make them valued companions in the tapestry of friendships.

Chapter Eighteen

Aries Challenges and Growth

A ries, like all zodiac signs, encounter challenges that shape their personal growth. With their fiery energy and bold approach to life, they are natural trailblazers, but this same intensity can sometimes present obstacles. Learning to navigate these hurdles allows Aries to channel their strengths more effectively and evolve into their best selves.

One of the most defining traits of Aries is their impulsive nature. They thrive on action, often making split-second decisions fueled by instinct rather than careful thought. While this trait brings excitement and spontaneity, it can also lead to missteps when they act before fully considering the consequences. Developing patience becomes an essential lesson for Aries. Learning to pause, reflect, and weigh their options before diving headfirst into situations can help them avoid unnecessary complications and cultivate a more strategic approach to life.

Their intense spirit also extends to their emotions, particularly when it comes to anger. Aries are passionate, and that passion can sometimes turn into frustration when things don't go their way. Quick-tempered outbursts may feel like a natural reaction, but finding healthy ways to manage their emotions is key to their growth. Practicing mindfulness, deep breathing, or channeling their energy into physical activity can help them maintain a sense of balance. Learning to respond rather than react allows them to maintain control without stifling their natural intensity.

While Aries are natural leaders, their strong-willed nature can make teamwork challenging. They often prefer to take charge and forge ahead rather than slow down to collaborate. However, life—whether in the workplace, relationships, or friendships—requires cooperation. Learning to value the perspectives of others, embrace compromise, and work within a team strengthens their ability to achieve success while fostering meaningful connections.

Their enthusiasm for new beginnings is unmatched. Aries are visionaries, always eager to embark on fresh projects, but sustaining momentum over the long haul can be difficult. They may find themselves losing interest or abandoning tasks when immediate excitement fades. Developing discipline and commitment allows Aries to follow through on their ambitions. Setting long-term goals and maintaining focus, even when faced with routine or challenges, can transform their natural drive into lasting achievement.

Communication is another area where Aries often face challenges. Their direct and assertive style leaves little room for subtlety, which can sometimes come across as blunt or tactless. While honesty is one of their greatest strengths, learning to temper it with diplomacy enhances their ability to navigate social situations. Understanding how their words impact others and choosing them carefully can strengthen relationships and prevent unnecessary conflict.

Balancing independence with collaboration is another significant area of growth. Aries take pride in their self-reliance and prefer to operate on their own terms. While this independence is a source of strength, recognizing when to seek help or share responsibilities can lead to even greater achievements. Knowing when to lead and when to lean on others creates a more harmonious balance in both personal and professional life.

Self-reflection is a skill that Aries may overlook in their fast-paced approach to life. Slowing down to evaluate their choices, behaviors, and motivations provides clarity and direction. Understanding their own strengths and weaknesses allows them to make more intentional decisions and refine their path forward.

Flexibility is another key lesson Aries must learn. Their determination and assertiveness drive them forward, but life is unpredictable. Not everything can be controlled, and sometimes plans need to change. Developing adaptability allows Aries to adjust without frustration, embracing challenges as opportunities rather than obstacles. Learning to flow with life's twists and turns rather than resisting them leads to a greater sense of peace and progress.

Recognizing these areas of growth empowers Aries to navigate life with greater wisdom and self-awareness. By embracing patience, refining their emotional responses, improving teamwork, strengthening commitment, and honing communication skills, they can transform their natural strengths into tools for success. Personal development is an ongoing journey, and for Aries, facing these challenges with their characteristic determination and resilience leads to a more balanced, fulfilling life.

Chapter Nineteen

Aries and Health

Aries vibrant energy and enthusiastic approach to life extends to their approach to health and well-being. Harnessing their natural vitality and maintaining a balanced lifestyle are key priorities for Aries.

Aries have a boundless reserve of energy that needs to be channeled effectively to ensure overall health and vitality. They thrive on physical activities and are often drawn to high-intensity exercises that get their adrenaline pumping. Engaging in activities such as running, martial arts, or competitive sports allows Aries to release excess energy and maintain their physical fitness. Regular exercise is essential for Aries to keep their bodies in peak condition and to prevent restlessness or pent-up energy from causing imbalances.

The above being said, Aries must also learn to balance their intense energy with rest and relaxation. As they can be prone to pushing themselves too hard, burnout and exhaustion can become a risk. It is crucial for Aries to incorporate restorative practices into their routine, such as meditation, deep breathing exercises, or gentle yoga. These activities help Aries reconnect with their inner selves, find calm amidst the chaos, and recharge their batteries.

In terms of diet, Aries benefit from foods that support their energy levels and provide the necessary fuel for their active lifestyles. A well-balanced diet with a focus on lean proteins, whole grains, and fresh fruits and vegetables is ideal for Aries. They should incorporate foods that promote brain function and mental clarity, such as fatty fish, nuts, and seeds. Aries should also be mindful of their tendency to rush through meals and practice mindful eating, savoring each bite and paying attention to their body's hunger and fullness cues.

Aries are prone to stress due to their ambitious nature and desire for constant action. To maintain their well-being, it is crucial for Aries to develop healthy stress-management techniques. Engaging in activities that promote relaxation, such as taking regular breaks, pursuing hobbies, or spending time in nature, can help Aries find balance and recharge their mental and emotional batteries. Aries can also benefit from learning and practicing mindfulness or meditation techniques to cultivate a sense of inner calm and reduce stress levels.

Maintaining emotional balance is also vital for Aries' overall health. Aries are known for their fiery temperament and can be prone to impulsiveness or impatience. Cultivating self-awareness and developing healthy coping mechanisms for managing anger or frustration is important for their emotional well-being. Aries can benefit from exploring practices like journaling, therapy, or engaging in creative outlets that allow them to express and process their emotions in a constructive manner.

Aries thrive on their abundant energy but must also prioritize maintaining balance in their health and well-being. By harnessing their energy through regular physical activity, finding moments of rest and relaxation, following a balanced diet, managing stress effectively, and cultivating emotional balance, Aries can optimize their health and lead fulfilling lives.

Understanding their unique needs and finding harmony within themselves is the key to Aries' overall well-being.

Chapter Twenty

Aries and Creativity

Aries possess a vibrant and dynamic creativity that fuels their passion for artistic expression. They are driven by an inner fire that ignites their imagination and compels them to explore various creative outlets. Aries approach creativity with enthusiasm, fearlessness, and an unwavering commitment to self-expression.

At the core of Aries' creativity is their boundless energy and adventurous spirit. They are not afraid to venture into uncharted territories, push boundaries, and take risks in their artistic pursuits. Aries thrive on the thrill of experimentation and the exhilaration of trying something new. They have an innate ability to infuse their artistic endeavors with a sense of vitality and spontaneity that captivates audiences.

Aries often have a distinct and recognizable artistic style that sets them apart. They have nurtured a natural sense of confidence and authenticity, which shines through in their creative works. Aries artists are unapologetically themselves, using their art as a medium to express their unique perspectives and make a bold statement. Their creativity is driven by a deep-seated need to share their vision with the world and leave a lasting impression.

Aries are known for their passion and dedication to their creative pursuits. They approach their art with a sense of urgency and purpose, pouring their heart and soul into every brushstroke, note, or word. Aries artists thrive in high-energy environments where they can fully immerse themselves in the creative process. They find inspiration in the fast-paced rhythm of life and channel their experiences and emotions into their artistic expressions.

Aries excel in a wide range of creative disciplines. Their versatility allows them to explore different art forms and mediums, constantly pushing the boundaries of their creativity. Whether it's painting, music, writing, acting, or any other form of artistic expression, Aries bring a sense of vitality and originality to their craft. They are not afraid to challenge conventions, break the rules, and create something entirely unique and groundbreaking.

The creative process for Aries is often characterized by bursts of inspiration and intense focus. They have a natural ability to tap into their artistic fire and channel it into their work. Aries thrive on the adrenaline rush that comes with creative breakthroughs and use these moments to fuel their momentum. They are driven by a deep desire to leave their mark on the world through their artistic endeavors.

Aries also possess strong leadership qualities, which often translate into their creative pursuits. They have a natural ability to take charge, organize, and bring a creative vision to life. Aries artists are often trailblazers, setting trends and pushing the boundaries of what is considered conventional in their respective art forms. They are not afraid to take the lead and inspire others with their artistic expression.

Aries embody a fiery and adventurous approach to creativity. They fearlessly explore new artistic territories, infuse their work with passion and authenticity, and leave a lasting impact through their unique artistic voice. Aries thrive on the energy and excitement of the creative process, constantly pushing boundaries and inspiring others with their artistic endeavors. Their creativity is a testament to their inner fire and an expression of their unwavering commitment to self-expression and artistic exploration.

Chapter Twenty-One

Famous Aries

Aries, the fiery and assertive zodiac sign ruled by Mars, has left an indelible mark on the world through the lives of numerous iconic individuals. The dynamic and pioneering spirit of Aries, characterized by ambition, courage, and leadership, has propelled these figures to remarkable achievements across various fields.

Leonardo da Vinci (April 15, 1452):

Leonardo da Vinci, the epitome of Renaissance brilliance, embodied the Aries spirit of innovation and creativity. His pioneering contributions to art, science, and engineering showcase the dynamic and visionary nature of Aries.

Maya Angelou (April 4, 1928):

Renowned poet and author Maya Angelou's life reflects the Aries qualities of resilience and fearlessness. Her impactful words and commitment to civil rights highlight the assertive and determined side of this fire sign.

Elton John (March 25, 1947):

Sir Elton John, an Aries music icon, epitomizes the sign's passion and flamboyance. His trailblazing career, marked by creativity and showmanship, mirrors the Aries drive to break boundaries in the world of music. Quite possibly, the greatest pop musician of all time.

Emma Watson (April 15, 1990):

Emma Watson, known for her role as Hermione Granger, represents the Aries commitment to justice and equality. Her advocacy for women's rights and education aligns with the sign's fearless pursuit of social change.

Vincent van Gogh (March 30, 1853):

Vincent van Gogh's tumultuous yet prolific artistic journey exemplifies the Aries spirit of passion and individuality. His expressive and emotionally charged works reveal the depth and intensity associated with this fire sign.

Lady Gaga (March 28, 1986):

Lady Gaga, a dynamic Aries performer, is known for her bold and innovative approach to music and fashion. Her fearless expression of individuality and creativity mirrors the adventurous and pioneering nature of Aries.

Leon Russell (April 2, 1942):

Leon Russell, a legendary figure in rock and roll, exemplifies the Aries penchant for originality and leadership. His influential contributions to music reflect the independent and trailblazing spirit of this fire sign.

Maya Moore (June 11, 1989):

Maya Moore's achievements on the basketball court and her advocacy for criminal justice reform embody the Aries drive for excellence and social impact. Her fearless pursuit of justice reflects Aries' courageous spirit.

Robert Downey Jr. (April 4, 1965):

Robert Downey Jr., known for his diverse roles in film, captures the Aries energy of versatility and charisma. His ability to reinvent himself and take on challenging roles aligns with the bold and dynamic nature of Aries.

Billie Holiday (April 7, 1915):

Billie Holiday's soulful and emotive voice in jazz music embodies the Aries passion for self-expression. Her influential contributions to the music industry showcase the intense and pioneering qualities associated with this fire sign.

Russell Crowe (April 7, 1964):

Russell Crowe's commanding presence and versatile acting skills reflect the Aries traits of leadership and determination. His impactful performances highlight the assertive and ambitious nature of this fire sign.

Sarah Jessica Parker (March 25, 1965):

Sarah Jessica Parker, best known for her role in "Sex and the City," embodies the Aries love for style and individuality. Her influence in fashion and entertainment reflects the dynamic and adventurous spirit of Aries.

The lives of these famous individuals touched by Aries illustrate the dynamic, pioneering, and fearless qualities associated with this fire sign. From the realms of art and literature to music and activism, these figures have harnessed the celestial energies of Aries to leave an enduring impact on the world.

Chapter Twenty-Two

Aries and Gemstones

Aries can enhance their natural strengths and attract good fortune by wearing certain gemstones believed to bring luck and amplify their positive qualities. These stones resonate with Aries' bold, energetic nature, offering support in different aspects of life, from ambition and success to emotional balance and protection.

Diamond, the birthstone of Aries, symbolizes strength, clarity, and invincibility. It mirrors Aries' fearless approach to life, enhancing their courage, ambition, and leadership abilities. Known for its association with prosperity and abundance, the diamond is believed to bring success in Aries' pursuits, reinforcing their natural determination and drive.

Ruby, often regarded as the king of gemstones, perfectly aligns with Aries' fiery spirit. It radiates passion, vitality, and courage, empowering Aries to pursue their goals with even greater intensity. This gemstone is believed to attract good fortune, wealth, and success while providing protection against negativity. It also enhances love and passion, strengthening both romantic and personal relationships.

Bloodstone is a powerful talisman for Aries, symbolizing resilience, physical strength, and endurance. Known for its protective properties, it shields against negative energies while boosting Aries' vitality. This stone is closely linked to luck, abundance, and success, making it a valuable companion for Aries in their endeavors, helping them push through obstacles with confidence and perseverance.

Carnelian resonates deeply with Aries' dynamic energy and ambition. Its warm, fiery hue reflects Aries' bold nature, inspiring motivation, creativity, and courage. This gemstone fuels their determination, helping them stay focused on their goals while also attracting luck and success. Carnelian is also associated with confidence, self-expression, and vitality, encouraging Aries to embrace their full potential.

Amethyst offers a calming balance to Aries' passionate and sometimes impulsive tendencies. It promotes clarity of thought, intuition, and spiritual awareness, helping Aries make wise decisions rather than acting purely on impulse. This gemstone attracts positive energy and protection while fostering emotional balance, inner strength, and a sense of peace amidst Aries' fast-paced lifestyle.

Garnet, a stone of passion and motivation, harmonizes with Aries' relentless drive. It fuels their determination, providing the energy and focus needed to accomplish their ambitions. Associated with abundance and prosperity, garnet enhances Aries' ability to manifest success while also strengthening personal relationships. It encourages love, devotion, and commitment, helping Aries cultivate deeper connections in both personal and professional life.

By incorporating these gemstones into their lives, Aries can harness their unique energies to enhance their strengths, attract luck, and maintain balance. Whether seeking success, protection, emotional harmony, or motivation, these stones serve as powerful allies, supporting Aries in their journey toward achievement and personal growth.

Chapter Twenty-Three

Aries Birthstone, Diamond

The diamond, the birthstone of Aries, is a gemstone of brilliance, strength, and timeless beauty. Its radiant energy aligns perfectly with Aries' bold and dynamic nature, offering both symbolic and practical benefits to those born under this fiery sign.

As one of the hardest substances on Earth, the diamond represents resilience and invincibility. Aries, known for their courage and determination, can draw upon its energy to reinforce their inner strength and fearlessness. It serves as a powerful reminder of their ability to rise above challenges, inspiring them to push forward with confidence and achieve their goals.

This gemstone also amplifies Aries' most admirable qualities—boldness, ambition, and leadership. The diamond enhances their natural charisma, empowering them to shine in their pursuits and leave a lasting impact. It magnifies confidence and courage, helping Aries attract success while maintaining their fearless approach to life.

Long associated with wealth and prosperity, the diamond is believed to attract financial opportunities and material blessings. Its energy aligns with Aries' enterprising spirit, helping them manifest abundance in their careers, investments, and personal endeavors. Whether striving for professional success or financial stability, Aries may find that the diamond serves as a beacon of good fortune.

While Aries possess boundless enthusiasm, they sometimes need greater clarity and focus to direct their energy effectively. The diamond is thought to sharpen mental clarity, providing a clear vision of their goals and helping them stay on course. It supports wise decision-making, encouraging thoughtful choices over impulsive actions, and strengthening Aries' ability to see opportunities with precision.

Emotional balance is another area where the diamond proves valuable. Aries' passionate and intense emotions can sometimes lead to impatience or restlessness. This gemstone is believed to bring harmony and inner peace, offering a stabilizing influence that helps Aries navigate their emotions with greater ease. It also carries associations with healing and purification, supporting their emotional well-being and encouraging a sense of calm.

Beyond personal growth and success, the diamond holds deep meaning in matters of love. Symbolizing eternal commitment, it enhances passion, loyalty, and connection in relationships. Aries, known for their fiery and adventurous approach to love, may find that the diamond strengthens their bonds, bringing joy and harmony to their romantic life.

While some Aries may feel a strong connection to the diamond's energy, others may resonate more with different gemstones or find meaning in a combination of birthstones. The choice is deeply personal, shaped by individual beliefs and experiences. Whether worn for its symbolism, aesthetic appeal, or spiritual benefits, the diamond stands as a powerful talisman, reflecting Aries' unwavering strength, brilliance, and boundless potential.

Aries Association with Symbols and Rituals

As the first sign of the zodiac, Aries is deeply connected to symbols and rituals that reflect their bold, energetic nature. These elements hold meaning for Aries, reinforcing their identity, strengths, and purpose while providing inspiration for their journey through life.

The ram stands as the most recognized symbol of Aries, embodying strength, courage, and assertiveness. Just as a ram fearlessly charges forward, Aries approach life with determination, embracing challenges head-on. This unwavering spirit fuels their natural leadership qualities and pioneering attitude, making the ram a powerful representation of their adventurous and ambitious personality.

Fire, the element associated with Aries, further illustrates their dynamic nature. Passionate, energetic, and full of enthusiasm, Aries radiate the intensity of a flame, sparking excitement in those around them. Fire symbolizes transformation and empowerment, mirroring Aries' drive to initiate change, take risks, and pursue their desires with relentless vigor. This element inspires them to embrace their boldest ambitions and ignite the world with their ideas.

The arrival of Aries each year aligns with the *Spring Equinox*, a time of renewal, growth, and new beginnings. Just as the Earth awakens from winter's slumber, Aries thrives in fresh starts, bringing an innate ability to embrace change and embark on new ventures. The energy of the equinox resonates deeply with Aries, reminding them of their potential to forge new paths, plant the seeds of innovation, and welcome the unknown with excitement.

A deep connection to their birthday fuels Aries' love for personal rituals, as they often see this occasion as a time of reflection and renewal. Many Aries engage in meditation, journaling, or vision board creation, using these practices to set intentions and channel their inner fire. These rituals allow them to realign with their passions, reaffirm their goals, and fuel their unstoppable drive for personal growth.

With a natural inclination toward competition, Aries find fulfillment in physical challenges and sports that test their limits. Their love for activity provides an outlet for their boundless energy, allowing them to showcase their leadership skills, determination, and unshakable will to win. Whether competing in a sport, engaging in a challenge, or pushing themselves to new heights, Aries thrives in environments that require stamina, resilience, and courage.

At their core, Aries are initiators—trailblazers who thrive on starting new projects, ventures, and groundbreaking ideas. Taking the lead is not just a preference but a fundamental part of their identity. They find purpose in exploring uncharted territory, introducing innovation, and fearlessly embracing new opportunities. For Aries, the act of initiating is a ritual in itself, reinforcing their need for independence, self-expression, and continuous evolution.

Each of these symbols and rituals serves as a reminder of Aries' vibrant nature, fueling their passion and reinforcing their innate strengths. By embracing these elements, Aries can harness their full potential, remain connected to their fiery spirit, and navigate life with confidence, courage, and an unyielding sense of purpose.

Chapter Twenty-Five

Aries' Lucky Plants

Astrology often links gemstones and birthstones with luck, but certain plants are also believed to bring good fortune, particularly for Aries. These plants are thought to resonate with the energy and characteristics of Aries, helping to attract positive vibes and success.

The Red-Hot Poker, with its striking red and orange blooms, is one plant associated with Aries. Its fiery colors symbolize passion, energy, and vitality, mirroring the dynamic nature of this zodiac sign. The plant is believed to infuse its surroundings with enthusiasm and positive energy, bringing luck and success to Aries.

Aloe vera, known for its healing qualities and resilience, is another plant that resonates with Aries. It represents strength and rejuvenation, qualities that align with the Aries spirit of bouncing back from challenges. Aloe vera is thought to provide protection and promote both physical and emotional well-being, making it a lucky plant for this sign.

Rosemary, an aromatic herb, is connected to clarity and focus, traits important for Aries as they pursue their goals. It's believed to enhance memory and mental sharpness, while also attracting positive energy and success. Rosemary is often seen as a plant that wards off negative influences, helping Aries stay on track.

Geraniums, with their bright and colorful blooms, symbolize friendship, joy, and positive relationships. These flowers are considered lucky for Aries because they promote emotional well-being and harmony in both personal and professional connections. They are thought to attract good luck and positive experiences in relationships, making them a great plant for this fiery sign.

Lemon balm, known for its calming and uplifting properties, is another herb that aligns with Aries' need for balance. It's believed to help reduce stress and foster relaxation, which is particularly important for Aries' often intense energy. Lemon balm is thought to attract positive energy, increase optimism, and support overall well-being.

The idea of lucky plants stems from cultural beliefs, symbolism, and personal associations. While the luckiness of these plants may vary from person to person, they are generally seen as bringing positive energy and success to Aries.

Chapter Twenty-Six

Aries and Personal Style: Fashion, Beauty, and Self-Expression

Aries are well-known for their fearless and self-assured outlook on life, and their personal style perfectly mirrors their fiery and dynamic essence. When it comes to fashion, beauty, and self-expression, Aries embrace the opportunity to make a resounding statement and stand out from the crowd.

In the fashion world, Aries are naturally drawn to bold and daring styles. They possess an innate fearlessness that emboldens them to venture into uncharted territories, exploring vibrant colors, distinctive patterns, and unconventional cuts. Aries fashionistas are trendsetters who eagerly keep their finger on the pulse of the latest fashion innovations, effortlessly displaying their individuality through their sartorial choices. They are particularly attracted to garments that emanate power, such as impeccably tailored blazers, sleek leather jackets, and eye-catching accessories. Aries also possess a strong affinity for sporty and athletic fashion, relishing the unrestricted movement and dynamic energy these ensembles provide.

Beauty is another universe where Aries radiate with their innate confidence. They have an inherent luminosity that exudes from within, a reflection of their self-assurance. Aries gravitate towards makeup looks that accentuate their best features, emphasizing the use of vibrant and daring hues. They fearlessly experiment with captivating eyeshadow shades, audacious lip colors, and bold winged eyeliner to create striking visual statements. In terms of hairstyling,

Aries opt for impactful choices, be it a chic and daring pixie cut or a voluminous and attention-grabbing mane. They fully embrace their natural beauty and utilize cosmetics and hairstyles as instruments of self-expression and empowerment.

At the heart of Aries' personal style lies the fundamental desire for self-expression. They employ their garments, accessories, and overall appearance as mediums to show their unique personality and make an indelible mark. Aries embody unapologetic confidence and an unwavering sense of self, and their fashion choices are a testament to this disposition. They effortlessly blend assorted styles and trends, concocting ensembles that are uniquely their own, effortlessly merging elements of high fashion with streetwear or vintage pieces. The distinctive personal style of Aries is accompanied by a commanding presence and innate magnetism that only serves to amplify their charismatic aura.

Aries approach fashion, beauty, and self-expression with a fearlessly audacious spirit. They relish in taking risks, fearlessly experimenting with vibrant colors and captivating patterns, all while leaving an indelible imprint through their unique sense of style. Their fashion choices seamlessly reflect their vivacious and self-assured nature, serving as a canvas for highlighting their individuality and magnetic personality. Fashion and beauty serve as powerful tools of self-expression for Aries, enabling them to embrace their inner fire and leave an indelible impression wherever their path may lead.

Chapter Twenty-Seven

Aries and Spirituality

S pirituality is a voyage of self-discovery and inner fortitude for Aries, embodying the essence of the warrior archetype. Aries approaches spirituality with unwavering determination and an innate longing to unravel the mysteries of existence while tapping into their inherent inner power.

The warrior energy that resides within Aries manifests itself in their spiritual path. They possess an innate curiosity and an unyielding drive to explore and confront life's challenges head-on. Aries fearlessly question conventional beliefs and norms, opting to forge their own distinct spiritual journey. Authenticity is paramount to them, and they actively seek experiences that ignite the flames within, pushing their boundaries to the very edge.

Aries discover solace and connect with the divine through physical and active practices. They are drawn to disciplines that demand discipline, courage, and endurance. Engaging in martial arts, vigorous yoga practices, or physically demanding rituals enables Aries to channel their energy and establish a profound connection with their spiritual essence. Through these practices, Aries taps into their inner strength and cultivates resilience and empowerment.

The spiritual odyssey of an Aries revolves around self-mastery and personal transformation. They understand the significance of conquering internal conflicts, facing fears, and embracing vulnerability. Aries recognize that true strength emanates not from domination or aggression but from their ability to harness their energy and align it with their highest intentions.

In matters of spirituality, Aries often adopt a direct and assertive approach. They fearlessly challenge spiritual doctrines and embark on unconventional paths. Aries embraces their individuality, ceaselessly striving to establish a unique connection with the divine. Exploring various belief systems, philosophies, and spiritual practices, Aries selects what resonates with their essence, discarding what does not. They possess a natural aptitude for carving their own spiritual path, finding profound meaning in firsthand experiences.

For Aries, spirituality is a ceaseless quest for truth and authenticity. They harbor a deep longing to comprehend their purpose and make a meaningful impact in the world. Aries often emerge as trailblazers, fearlessly forging new paths and inspiring others with their unyielding determination. Their spirituality serves as a catalyst for personal growth and self-empowerment, allowing them to tap into their innate potential and lead with unwavering courage and conviction.

Aries approach spirituality as the *warrior's expedition* towards inner strength. They wholeheartedly embrace their role as seekers, fearlessly exploring unconventional realms and challenging established beliefs. By engaging in physical and active practices, Aries taps into their wellspring of inner power and cultivates resilience. Their spiritual journey is characterized by self-mastery, personal transformation, and authentic self-expression. Aries shine as trailblazers, carving their unique path and inspiring others to embrace their own spiritual truths.

Chapter Twenty-Eight

Aries and Finance

Aries bring their characteristic boldness and ambition to their approach to money matters. They possess a natural drive and determination to achieve financial success and are not afraid to take risks when it comes to their finances. Aries have a desire to be financially independent and to have control over their wealth.

Aries tend to have a proactive and assertive attitude towards money. They are not afraid to pursue opportunities, negotiate deals, and assert their value in financial transactions. Aries have a natural ability to take the lead and make bold financial decisions, often with a focus on long-term growth and wealth accumulation.

Aries are known for their entrepreneurial spirit and their ability to seize opportunities. They are often drawn to careers or business ventures that allow them to exercise their leadership skills and take charge of their financial destiny. They thrive in dynamic and competitive environments, where they can use their natural instincts to make shrewd financial moves and create wealth.

When it comes to wealth management, Aries are typically proactive and hands-on. They prefer to have a clear understanding of their financial situation and take an active role in managing their assets. Aries are not afraid to seek advice from financial experts or engage in self-education to improve their financial knowledge and decision-making skills.

Aries have a natural inclination towards taking calculated risks with their investments. They are willing to venture into new and emerging markets, explore unconventional investment opportunities, and think freely when it comes to growing their wealth. Aries have a high tolerance for risk and are willing to embrace volatility in pursuit of potentially higher returns.

However, Aries should be cautious not to let their impulsive nature or impatience interfere with their financial decisions. It is important for them to carefully evaluate their options, conduct thorough research, and seek advice when needed to ensure that their financial choices align with their long-term goals.

In terms of spending habits, Aries enjoy indulging in the finer things in life and are not afraid to spend on experiences or items that bring them joy and pleasure. They value quality and are willing to invest in products or services that enhance their lifestyle. However, they should also be mindful of maintaining a balance between their desires and their financial responsibilities.

Overall, Aries approach money matters with confidence, ambition, and a proactive mindset. They have a natural inclination towards entrepreneurship, a willingness to take calculated risks, and a desire for financial independence. With careful planning, informed decision-making, and a focus on long-term growth, Aries have the potential to build substantial wealth and achieve their financial goals.

Spells Tailored for Aries

As a fiery and dynamic sign, Aries individuals may be drawn to spells and rituals that reflect their energetic and assertive nature. While there are no specific spells or rituals exclusively for Aries, there are certain practices and intentions that align with their characteristics and can enhance their personal growth and manifestation abilities.

New Beginnings Ritual

Aries thrive on fresh starts and new beginnings. Performing a ritual to mark the start of a new phase, such as a new year, a new project, or a personal transformation, can be powerful for Aries. This ritual may involve setting intentions, writing down goals, and symbolically letting go of anything that no longer serves them. Lighting a red or orange candle, which represents the fire element associated with Aries, can help ignite their energy and passion for their new journey.

A Wiccan New Beginnings Spell is a ritual performed to mark the start of a new chapter in life, whether it's the beginning of a new year, a fresh start after a challenging period, or the initiation of a new project or phase. This spell aims to harness the energies of renewal, transformation, and growth to bring positive changes and opportunities into your life. It is a powerful tool for setting intentions, manifesting new beginnings, and welcoming positive energy. Here are the ingredients and instructions for a basic Wiccan New Beginnings Spell:

Ingredients:

White candle (symbolizing purity, clarity, and new beginnings)

Green candle (symbolizing growth, abundance, and prosperity)

A small bowl of water

A small bowl of salt

A piece of paper or parchment

Pen or marker

Fresh flowers or herbs (symbolizing renewal and new growth)
Optional: Crystals or gemstones associated with new beginnings (such as clear quartz or moonstone)

Preparation

- Find a quiet and sacred space where you can perform the spell without distractions.

- Set up your altar or clean surface with your materials.

- Take a moment to center yourself and reflect on the new beginning you wish to manifest.

Setting Your Intention

- Light the white candle, symbolizing purity and clarity.

- Hold your hands over the candle flame and state your intention for the new beginning, such as: "I embrace this new chapter in my life. May it be filled with growth, abundance, and positive opportunities."

Elemental Purification

- Take the bowl of water and sprinkle a few drops over your hands, symbolizing the purifying and cleansing properties of water.

- Say: "With this water, I cleanse and purify myself, releasing any past energies that no longer serve my journey."

Symbolic Purification

- Take a pinch of salt from the bowl and sprinkle it over the piece of paper or parchment.

- Visualize the salt purifying the paper and removing any obstacles or negative energies.

- Say: "With this salt, I cleanse and purify my path, removing any barriers and inviting positive energies for new beginnings."

Written Intention:

Write down your intention for the new beginning on the piece of paper or parchment. Be specific and clear in stating your desires, focusing on positive and empowering language. For example: "I welcome new opportunities for personal growth, abundance, and happiness in my life. I am open to positive change and new beginnings."

Candle Activation

Light the green candle, symbolizing growth, abundance, and prosperity. Hold the piece of paper with your written intention and pass it through the flame of the green candle, infusing it with the energy of new beginnings. Visualize your intention manifesting as the flame ignites the transformative power within you.

Floral Offering

Arrange the fresh flowers or herbs on your altar or hold them in your hands. Close your eyes and connect with the vibrant energy of the flowers, envisioning them as symbols of renewal and new growth. Offer the flowers or herbs to the elements, expressing gratitude for the new beginnings you are welcoming.

Crystal Energy (Optional):

If you have chosen crystals or gemstones associated with new beginnings, hold them in your hands or place them on your altar.

Visualize the crystals radiating their energy of transformation and positive change, amplifying your intentions.

Affirmation and Visualization:

Hold the piece of paper with your intention in both hands and read it aloud, infusing it with your energy and conviction. Close your eyes and visualize yourself stepping into the new beginning, feeling the excitement, growth, and abundance that it brings. Repeat a positive affirmation aligned with your intention, such as: "I embrace new beginnings with open arms. I am ready to receive the blessings that come my way."

Closing the Ritual

Express gratitude to the divine forces, the elements, and any deities or guides you invoked. Allow the candles to burn out safely or snuff them out, while expressing your thanks and releasing the energy into the universe. Keep the piece of paper with your intention in a safe place or carry it with you as a reminder of your new beginnings.

The Wiccan New Beginnings Spell is a powerful way to set intentions, manifest positive changes, and invite new opportunities into your life. Embrace the energy of renewal, growth, and transformation as you embark on your new journey. Trust in the power of your intentions and the support of the universe to guide you towards a bright and prosperous future.

Courage and Confidence Spell

Aries are known for their courage and confidence. A spell focused on enhancing these qualities can be empowering for them. This spell may involve visualizing a strong and confident version of themselves, reciting affirmations that boost self-esteem, and carrying a crystal such as carnelian or citrine, which are associated with courage and confidence. Aries individuals can personalize the spell to suit their needs and intentions, using their assertiveness and determination to infuse the spell with their fiery energy.

The Wiccan self-confidence spell is a ritual designed to help individuals enhance their self-esteem and develop a positive sense of self-worth. It aims to empower individuals and cultivate a deep belief in their abilities and worthiness. Here is a full description of the Wiccan self-confidence spell:

Ingredients:

White candle

Small mirror

Piece of paper

Pen or marker

Essential oil (optional)

Incense (optional)

Clear quartz crystal (optional)

Preparation:

- Find a quiet and comfortable space where you can perform the spell without interruptions.

- Cleanse and purify the space by burning incense or using any method that resonates with you.

- Gather all the ingredients and place them within reach.

Setting Intentions:

Take a few deep breaths to ground yourself and focus your mind. Light the white candle, symbolizing purity and clarity of intention. Hold the mirror in your hands and visualize radiant confidence and self-assuredness filling your being. State your intention clearly, such as "I am worthy, confident, and deserving of all the good things in my life."

Writing Affirmations:

Take the piece of paper and write down positive affirmations about yourself and your abilities. Choose statements that resonate with you and reflect the qualities you want to embody. Examples could be: "I am confident and capable," "I embrace my uniqueness and shine my light," or "I am worthy of love and success." Write them in the present tense, as if they are already true.

Empowering the Affirmations:

Read each affirmation aloud, allowing the words to resonate within you. Envision yourself embodying each affirmation, feeling the confidence and self-assurance growing within you. As you read each affirmation, visualize the words being absorbed into the mirror, infusing it with positive energy.

Charging the Mirror:

If desired, anoint the mirror with a few drops of essential oil that enhances confidence, such as rosemary or bergamot. Hold the mirror up to the candle flame, allowing the light to reflect onto the mirror's surface. Visualize the mirror absorbing the empowering energy from the flame, becoming a powerful tool for self-reflection and confidence.

Affirmation Activation:

Hold the mirror in front of you and investigate your own reflection. Repeat each affirmation aloud, gazing into your own eyes and allowing the words to sink deeply into your subconscious. Feel the energy of confidence and self-assurance radiating from the mirror and into your being.

Closing the Ritual:

Express gratitude to the Universe, the Divine, or any deities or spirits you work with for their guidance and support. Snuff out the candle, acknowledging the end of the ritual and the beginning of your empowered journey. Keep the mirror and the affirmations in a safe place, using them as reminders of your self-confidence whenever needed.

The power of any spell lies within your intentions and belief. The Wiccan self-confidence spell is a tool to help you tap into your inner strength and cultivate a positive mindset. Embrace the process with an open heart and mind, and trust in your own abilities to manifest self-confidence and empowerment.

Passion and Creativity Ritual

Aries men and women have a natural passion and creative spark. They can enhance these qualities through a ritual that nurtures their creative spirit. This ritual may involve engaging in activities that inspire them, such as writing, painting, or dancing. They can also create an altar dedicated to their creative endeavors, adorned with symbols and items that ignite their passion. Incorporating red, which symbolizes passion and vitality, can amplify the energy of the ritual.

A Wiccan Creativity Spell is a ritual performed to enhance your creative abilities, unlock inspiration, and tap into your artistic potential. This spell aims to connect you with the divine source of creativity, remove blocks or self-doubt, and ignite your imagination. Whether you are an artist, writer, musician, or simply seeking to enhance your creative expression, this spell can help you access your creative flow. Here are the ingredients and instructions for a basic Wiccan

Creativity Spell

Ingredients:

Purple candle (representing inspiration, intuition, and artistic energy)

Creative tools or materials relevant to your chosen artistic medium (e.g., paintbrushes, musical instrument, writing journal)

Clear quartz crystal

Jasmine or lavender essential oil (or dried jasmine or lavender flowers)

Altar or sacred space

Preparation

- Find a quiet and sacred space where you can perform the spell without distractions.

- Set up your altar or clean surface with your materials.

- Take a moment to center yourself and focus on your desire to enhance your creativity and artistic expression.

Setting Your Intention

Hold the creative tools or materials in your hands and connect with the energy of your chosen artistic medium. Visualize yourself immersed in a state of creative flow, feeling inspired and connected to your inner artist. State your intention for the spell, either silently or aloud, such as: "I unlock my creative potential and invite inspiration to flow freely."

Candle Preparation

Light the purple candle, symbolizing inspiration, intuition, and artistic energy. Hold the candle in your hands, infusing it with your intention and the energy of creative expression. State your intention for the spell, either silently or aloud, focusing on your desire to enhance your creativity.

Crystal Activation

Hold the clear quartz crystal in your hands. Close your eyes and imagine the crystal amplifying your creative energy and connecting you with the divine source of inspiration. Envision it as a conduit for channeling artistic ideas and expressions.

Scent Activation

If you have jasmine or lavender essential oil, place a drop on your fingertips and gently rub them together. If you have dried jasmine or lavender flowers, hold them in your hands and take a moment to connect with their calming and inspiring properties. Inhale the scent of jasmine or lavender, allowing it to relax your mind and stimulate your senses.

Creative Invocation

Take your creative tools or materials and set them before the lit candle. Close your eyes and visualize a radiant purple light surrounding you and your creative space. Call upon the divine source of creativity and any artistic deities or spirits you resonate with, inviting their guidance and inspiration.

Creative Expression

Pick up your creative tools or materials and allow your intuition to guide your artistic expression. Engage in your chosen artistic activity, whether it's painting, playing music, writing, or any other creative endeavor. Let go of self-judgment or perfectionism and allow the energy to flow naturally.

Affirmations

As you create, repeat positive affirmations related to your creativity and artistic abilities. For example: "I am a vessel of divine inspiration," "My creativity flows effortlessly and abundantly," or "I embrace my unique artistic expression."

Crystal Charging

Place the clear quartz crystal near your creative workspace or hold it in your hand as you continue your creative process. Visualize the crystal absorbing the energy of your creative flow, amplifying your inspiration, and helping you bring forth your best artistic expression.

Closing the Ritual

Express gratitude to yourself, the divine, or any artistic deities or spirits you called upon, acknowledging their support and the creative energy you have invoked. Allow the candle to burn out naturally or extinguish it while expressing gratitude and releasing the energy into the universe.

A Wiccan Creativity Spell is a tool to enhance your creative energy, but the true power lies within you. Embrace your unique artistic expression and trust in your creative abilities. Combine this spell with regular creative practices, seeking inspiration from nature and other artists, and nurturing your creativity through self-care and self-expression. Trust in the power of your intention and the support of the universe as you tap into your creative flow and unleash your artistic potential.

Chapter Thirty

Compatibility Between Aries and Aries

Exploring the compatibility between two Aries individuals, who share the same zodiac sign, can be an exciting yet challenging experience. Both possess an abundance of energy, passion, and enthusiasm, which fosters a dynamic and thrilling connection. They motivate each other, embarking on new adventures and eagerly pursuing their goals together.

Aries are known for their assertiveness, confidence, independence, and courage. These similar traits help them understand each other deeply, creating a sense of camaraderie and mutual respect. This shared personality creates a strong foundation, where both partners can connect and support each other's ambitions.

However, Aries also have a competitive nature. While this drive fuels personal growth and ambition, it can sometimes trigger power struggles and conflicts within the relationship. Striking a balance between healthy competition and conflict management becomes crucial, as excessive rivalry could harm the partnership.

Being passionate individuals, Aries are prone to quick tempers, and arguments can escalate quickly. This fiery temperament means that effective communication and constructive anger management are key to maintaining harmony. Both partners must be aware of the potential for intense disagreements and focus on avoiding destructive patterns.

Another important aspect of the Aries- Aries relationship is their shared need for independence. Both value personal space and freedom, so respecting each other's autonomy is essential. Finding a healthy balance between togetherness and individuality will help maintain a strong and harmonious connection.

Despite their competitive nature, Aries are fiercely supportive of one another. They understand each other's drive and determination, offering encouragement and serving as each other's cheerleaders. This mutual support helps both individuals stay motivated, even when facing challenges.

Since Aries thrive on excitement and novelty, keeping the spark alive in the relationship requires effort. Engaging in new activities and creating shared experiences ensures that the relationship remains fresh and adventurous, avoiding feelings of boredom or stagnation.

The compatibility between two Aries depends on their ability to respect and understand each other's needs. By maintaining open communication, mutual respect, and a commitment to personal growth, they can navigate challenges and build a passionate, fiery partnership.

Chapter Thirty-One

Compatibility Between Aries and Taurus

The compatibility between Aries and Taurus presents a fascinating combination of fiery passion and grounded stability. These two signs, though different in many ways, complement each other in numerous surprising ways. Aries, a fire sign, brings boundless energy and enthusiasm, known for their dynamic, go-getter attitude. In contrast, Taurus, an earth sign, offers stability and determination, providing a grounding influence that balances Aries' drive. Together, they form a harmonious dynamic, where each brings something essential to the relationship.

Aries' assertiveness and confidence are key aspects of their personality, as they express their desires and opinions directly. On the other hand, Taurus is more practical and patient, offering a sensibility that helps temper Aries' impulsiveness. Taurus' presence acts as a stabilizing force in the relationship, grounding Aries' sometimes scattered energy.

While Aries thrives on excitement and adventure, seeking spontaneity and new experiences, Taurus values security, comfort, and stability. This difference in priorities creates a balance, as Taurus offers a sense of security, supporting Aries' need for adventure while ensuring that both partners feel safe and nurtured. Their relationship blends the thrill of exploration with the comfort of stability.

Communication between Aries and Taurus can be a bit of a challenge, as their styles differ. Aries tends to be direct and straightforward, while Taurus takes a more patient and reflective approach. To avoid misunderstandings, it's essential for both to find a balance, with Aries learning to embrace patience and Taurus becoming more open to directness.

When it comes to conflict resolution, Aries can be quick to anger, driven by their passionate nature, whereas Taurus remains calm and patient. Taurus' grounded approach helps diffuse heated situations, providing stability. Both partners will need to develop effective conflict resolution skills, finding common ground to maintain harmony in the relationship.

The complementary strengths between Aries and Taurus create a powerful partnership. Aries' boldness and willingness to take risks inspire Taurus to step out of their comfort zone, while Taurus' determination helps bring Aries' ideas to fruition. This mutual support creates a balanced dynamic where both can thrive.

Each partner has much to learn from the other. Aries can appreciate Taurus' patient, methodical approach to life, recognizing the value of stability and long-term planning. Conversely, Taurus can be inspired by Aries' adventurous spirit, learning to embrace new experiences and take more risks for personal growth.

Physically, Aries and Taurus often experience a strong attraction. Aries' passion and intensity mesh well with Taurus' sensuality and need for physical affection. This connection strengthens their emotional bond, deepening their relationship.

Building trust is essential in any relationship, and Aries and Taurus are no different. Taurus' reliability and loyalty provide Aries with the security they need, while Aries' openness and honesty help foster trust in Taurus. With patience and consistent effort, they can build a lasting foundation of trust.

In their relationship, finding a balance between independence and togetherness is crucial. Aries values personal freedom and independence, while Taurus seeks shared routines and closeness. By respecting each other's need for individuality while nurturing their bond, they can maintain a healthy relationship that honors both partners' desires.

In conclusion, the compatibility between Aries and Taurus is a blend of passion, stability, and growth. By embracing each other's unique qualities and understanding their respective needs, they can create a relationship filled with excitement, security, and a profound emotional connection.

Chapter Thirty-Two

Compatibility Between Aries and Gemini

Aries and Gemini share an intriguing blend of fiery energy and intellectual curiosity, making their compatibility both dynamic and engaging. Their communication skills are a strong point, as both excel at engaging in lively, stimulating conversations. They enjoy exchanging ideas, debating various topics, and appreciating each other's perspectives, which fosters a robust mental connection and a deep mutual understanding.

A natural sense of adventure unites Aries and Gemini, with both seeking new experiences and enjoying diverse activities. Their shared thirst for excitement leads them to embark on spontaneous adventures, encouraging each other to step out of their comfort zones. This sense of adventure adds a thrill and spontaneity to their relationship.

The playful dynamic between Aries and Gemini brings a youthful energy to their connection. Their quick-wittedness allows them to tease and banter, filling their time together with laughter and joy. This lightheartedness infuses their relationship with a sense of fun.

Intellectually, the two signs are perfectly matched. Aries and Gemini both have a strong appreciation for mental stimulation, enjoying deep conversations and the exchange of ideas. With Gemini's diverse interests complementing Aries' passionate nature, they create a balance that encourages the exploration of new thoughts and the expansion of their intellectual horizons.

Both Aries and Gemini value their independence and freedom, which allows them to maintain a sense of self within the relationship. They respect each other's need for personal space and individual pursuits, which helps create a healthy, balanced dynamic. Their independent natures complement one another, ensuring a relationship that honors both partners' need for autonomy.

Gemini's adaptability plays an important role in their compatibility with Aries. While Aries is often determined and occasionally headstrong, Gemini's flexible approach helps diffuse potential conflicts. At the same time, Aries' drive provides direction and motivation for Gemini, encouraging both partners' personal growth and supporting each other's ambitions.

Socially, Aries and Gemini thrive in the company of others. They enjoy attending parties, events, and gatherings together, as their shared extroverted nature creates a vibrant social life. They enjoy each other's company in various social contexts, making their relationship lively and engaging.

Gemini's love for variety brings freshness and excitement to their relationship, which Aries finds stimulating. They continuously explore new aspects of their connection, seeking ways to keep the passion alive and avoid falling into monotony. This drive for variety ensures that their relationship remains exciting and full of surprises.

However, both Aries and Gemini may face challenges when it comes to commitment. Their shared zest for life can make it difficult to settle into routines or focus on long-term commitments. Open communication about desires and expectations is essential for finding common ground and ensuring a shared vision for their future.

In the end, the compatibility between Aries and Gemini is a fusion of passionate energy, intellectual stimulation, and a shared sense of adventure. With effective communication, mutual respect, and a willingness to embrace each other's individuality, they can build a vibrant and intellectually engaging partnership.

Compatibility Between Aries and Cancer

Aries and Cancer, despite their contrasting qualities, have the potential for a unique and enriching relationship. Aries, with their fiery energy, brings excitement and passion, while Cancer offers a nurturing and compassionate presence. Together, they form a dynamic duo that balances adventure with emotional support, each complementing the other's strengths.

One of the main dynamics between Aries and Cancer is their differing needs for independence and emotional connection.

Aries values their independence, while Cancer craves emotional security and closeness. Finding a balance between these needs is crucial. Aries can learn to provide the reassurance that Cancer desires, while Cancer can encourage Aries to open up emotionally and express their feelings more freely.

In their relationship, Aries and Cancer also help each other grow. Aries can teach Cancer to be more assertive and confident, taking risks without hesitation, while Cancer can show Aries the importance of emotional intelligence, intuition, and nurturing. Their relationship helps them evolve into more well-rounded individuals, learning valuable lessons along the way.

Their emotional intimacy is another area where they connect deeply. Cancer's sensitivity and emotional depth resonate with Aries' passionate nature, and they find a safe space to share their feelings. Aries can help Cancer break out of their shell and experience the thrill of taking emotional risks, while Cancer offers Aries the comfort of emotional security. This creates an emotional connection that can be both intense and profound.

At times, though, their approach to conflict may clash. Aries tends to be direct and assertive, while Cancer is more sensitive and indirect. For their relationship to flourish, both partners need to work on communication and understanding, making an effort to bridge the gap between their differing styles. Cancer's empathy and Aries' willingness to compromise are key to resolving disagreements and preventing lingering resentment.

When it comes to building a home, Aries and Cancer each bring something different to the table. Cancer desires a stable, comfortable home, while Aries seeks excitement and novelty. Together, they strike a balance between creating a warm, nurturing sanctuary and inviting adventure into their lives. Their home can become a place of both comfort and excitement, blending their unique strengths.

As a couple, Aries and Cancer form a supportive partnership. Cancer's nurturing nature aligns well with Aries' ambitious drive, providing unwavering encouragement. At the same time, Aries inspires Cancer to pursue their own goals and dreams, creating a dynamic where both are motivated to achieve individually and as a couple.

While Cancer's emotional sensitivity and Aries' directness may sometimes cause tension, both partners can learn to navigate these differences. Aries must work on communicating with tact, while Cancer should make an effort to understand Aries' need for personal space. Empathy and open-mindedness are crucial to building a strong understanding between them.

Trust and emotional security are at the heart of their relationship. Cancer values loyalty and security, while Aries' honesty helps build the trust Cancer seeks. With time and consistent effort, they can establish a deep, unbreakable bond based on mutual trust and support.

Family life is another area where both Aries and Cancer connect. While Cancer cherishes family bonds and traditions, Aries focuses on bringing excitement and adventure to family life. By combining their strengths, they can create a loving and vibrant family environment that nurtures both stability and adventure.

In the end, the compatibility between Aries and Cancer is a blend of passion, nurturing, and emotional depth. Through understanding, compromise, and a shared commitment to personal growth, they can build a relationship that embraces both adventure and emotional connection, grounded in profound mutual support.

Chapter Thirty-Four

Compatibility Between Aries and Leo

Compatibility between Aries and Leo is a dynamic and passionate combination, bringing together two powerful and confident personalities. Both are fire signs, which means they share an abundance of energy, enthusiasm, and a zest for life. Their vibrant personalities create an instant spark, igniting a flame that fuels their relationship with passion and excitement.

Both Aries and Leo are natural-born leaders who thrive in the spotlight. They possess strong personalities, charisma, and a desire to take charge. Together, they form a power couple capable of accomplishing remarkable things, inspiring others with their ambition and determination. This leadership dynamic is paired with a deep mutual admiration. Aries is captivated by Leo's regal presence, confidence, and magnetic charm, while Leo is drawn to Aries' courage, assertiveness, and unyielding spirit. This respect for each other's strengths fuels their connection, enhancing their compatibility.

Their shared passions further bond them, as both Aries and Leo love excitement, adventure, and taking risks. Whether embarking on spontaneous trips or pursuing daring endeavors, they enjoy engaging in thrilling activities that push boundaries. This desire for exhilaration is matched by their creativity. Aries and Leo both possess a natural flair for self-expression, and when they come together, their creative energies merge. Their collaboration leads to dynamic and inspiring endeavors, with both supporting each other's artistic pursuits.

Their relationship is also characterized by assertiveness and confidence. Both Aries and Leo are unafraid to express their desires and opinions, and their direct communication style complements one another. They engage in open and honest conversations, addressing any issues with clarity and transparency. A healthy sense of competition also exists between them, motivating them to reach their full potential. This competitive spirit challenges them to strive for excellence, encouraging both personal growth and accomplishment within their relationship.

Their larger-than-life personalities bring a sense of drama and excitement, adding a spark to their connection. They enjoy being the center of attention and love creating memorable moments together. This theatrical nature keeps their romance alive, adding glamour to their lives. Loyalty and support are another foundation of their relationship. Aries and Leo are fiercely loyal, standing by each other through thick and thin. Their unwavering commitment creates a solid foundation for a lasting and fulfilling relationship.

However, both Aries and Leo have strong egos, which can occasionally lead to clashes. Despite this, their shared passion and mutual respect help them find a balance, allowing them to appreciate each other's individuality. They understand the importance of compromise and learn to set aside their egos for the sake of their relationship.

In the end, compatibility between Aries and Leo is an exciting fusion of passion, confidence, and shared aspirations. Their dynamic connection fuels their journey together, where they celebrate each other's strengths, inspire one another, and embrace a life full of adventure and fulfillment.

Chapter Thirty-Five

Compatibility Between Aries and Virgo

At first glance, the compatibility between Aries and Virgo may seem unlikely, but beneath their surface differences lies the potential for a balanced and harmonious relationship. Aries is bold, assertive, and ambitious, while Virgo is practical, organized, and attentive to detail. Together, they create a harmonious balance between action and analysis, enabling them to achieve their goals effectively.

There is much for both Aries and Virgo to learn from one another. Aries can inspire Virgo to embrace spontaneity, adventure, and risk-taking, while Virgo can teach Aries the importance of patience, precision, and practicality. They challenge each other to grow in areas where they may be less inclined.

Both Aries and Virgo have sharp intellects and enjoy engaging in stimulating conversations. They approach problem-solving differently: Aries relies on intuition and quick decision-making, while Virgo favors analysis and critical thinking. This intellectual compatibility facilitates deep discussions and the exchange of diverse perspectives, enhancing their connection.

The partnership between Aries and Virgo can be one of support and encouragement. Aries' enthusiasm and ambition motivate Virgo to pursue their goals, while Virgo's practicality and attention to detail provide valuable guidance and support for Aries' endeavors. Despite their differing approaches to life, they can develop a profound respect for each other's unique qualities. Aries appreciates Virgo's reliability, practicality, and strong work ethic, while Virgo admires Aries' confidence, assertiveness, and ability to take charge. This mutual respect strengthens their bond and fosters admiration.

Finding balance is essential in their relationship. Aries' impulsive nature contrasts with Virgo's cautious, analytical thinking. Striking a balance between Aries' spontaneity and Virgo's need for stability is crucial. By understanding and appreciating each other's perspectives, they can create a relationship that combines excitement with practicality.

Their communication styles may also differ. Aries tends to be direct and straightforward, while Virgo is more reserved and thoughtful. Patience and understanding are key to bridging these communication gaps and avoiding misunderstandings. By actively listening and valuing each other's viewpoints, they can foster effective communication, which is vital to the success of their relationship.

Both Aries and Virgo value loyalty, integrity, and hard work. They are committed partners who prioritize the well-being of their relationship, and their shared values create a base for trust and security within their partnership. Virgo's caring and nurturing nature creates a stable, emotionally supportive environment for Aries. In turn, Aries brings excitement, passion, and encouragement to Virgo's life, helping them experience the joys of spontaneity and taking risks.

Through shared experiences, challenges, and mutual support, Aries and Virgo can grow and evolve as a couple. Their relationship becomes a catalyst for personal growth and self-improvement, helping them become more well-rounded individuals. The compatibility between Aries and Virgo is a unique blend of contrasting qualities that, when embraced and understood, can create a fulfilling partnership. With open communication, mutual respect, and a willingness to learn from each other, they can build a relationship that combines action, practicality, and personal growth.

Chapter Thirty-Six

Compatibility Between Aries and Libra

Aries and Libra share an intriguing compatibility, blending fiery passion with harmonious balance. Despite their distinct qualities, their contrasting attributes create a dynamic and complementary relationship. Aries' boldness is irresistibly combined with Libra's charm, sparking a thrilling connection filled with intensity and excitement. This initial chemistry leads to a passionate and engaging relationship.

Aries is driven by ambition, independence, and a thirst for action, embodying the fire element, while Libra, as an air sign, represents balance, harmony, and diplomacy. Together, they create a yin-yang dynamic, with Aries bringing enthusiasm and drive while Libra contributes peace and equilibrium. Their energies complement one another, resulting in a well-rounded partnership.

Both Aries and Libra possess sharp intellects and enjoy engaging in stimulating conversations. Aries tends to be direct, while Libra adopts a more diplomatic approach. Their intellectual compatibility fosters lively debates, the exploration of ideas, and an enriching exchange of knowledge. Aries excels in leadership, taking initiative, and making quick decisions, while Libra shines in diplomacy, negotiation, and maintaining balance. Together, they form a powerful duo, combining Aries' assertiveness with Libra's ability to create harmony.

As social beings, Aries and Libra thrive together in various social settings. They enjoy attending parties, events, and gatherings, where their shared extroverted nature allows them to cultivate a vibrant social life. Their compatibility extends beyond private moments to create a rich, energetic social connection.

Both signs cherish values such as justice, fairness, and equality, striving to create a just and balanced world. These shared values provide a solid foundation for their relationship, enabling them to collaborate and pursue common goals. Over time, Aries and Libra develop a deep respect for each other's qualities. Aries admires Libra's ability to consider multiple perspectives and foster harmony, while Libra appreciates Aries' passion, determination, and unwavering drive. This mutual respect strengthens their bond and fosters admiration.

While both Aries and Libra highly value their independence, they understand and respect each other's need for personal space. This allows them to maintain their individuality while staying committed to the relationship, fostering a healthy and balanced dynamic. Aries' direct and assertive approach to conflict may sometimes clash with Libra's preference for peace, but both signs share a natural inclination for fairness and justice. By working together, they can find compromises and solutions that satisfy both parties, promoting effective conflict resolution and growth in their relationship.

Libra's ability to find balance helps temper Aries' impulsive nature. Libra encourages Aries to consider different perspectives and make more thoughtful decisions, while Aries inspires Libra to act and assert their needs when necessary. Together, they can create a balanced relationship that incorporates both spontaneity and harmony.

The compatibility between Aries and Libra is a blend of passion, intellectual stimulation, and a desire for balance and harmony. Through effective communication, mutual respect, and a willingness to embrace their unique qualities, they can cultivate a relationship that thrives on excitement, harmony, and personal growth.

Compatibility Between Aries and Scorpio

The compatibility between Aries and Scorpio is a powerful and intense combination, driven by passion, strength, and a deep connection. Despite their distinct qualities, their complementary traits and shared determination create a magnetic and transformative bond. Their chemistry is undeniable, and when they come together, sparks fly. Both signs are known for their intensity, and their physical attraction is potent, igniting a fiery connection that leads to a deeply fulfilling relationship.

Aries and Scorpio are both incredibly determined, with an unwavering drive to pursue their goals. Aries brings a bold and assertive nature, while Scorpio adds depth, focus, and emotional resilience. Together, they form a dynamic duo capable of conquering challenges and overcoming obstacles with their combined strength and tenacity. This shared determination fuels their relationship, helping them navigate any difficulties that arise.

Emotional depth is another key element of their connection. While Aries is direct and assertive with their emotions, Scorpio tends to be more mysterious and reserved. Despite these differences, both signs share a passionate and transformative nature that allows them to understand and connect with each other on a profound emotional level. This emotional depth strengthens their bond and creates a foundation for mutual understanding.

Trust and loyalty are crucial in this relationship. Both Aries and Scorpio value loyalty and are fiercely protective of their loved ones. Once trust is established, their bond becomes unbreakable. Aries' honesty and Scorpio's intuition create a solid foundation of trust, enabling them to be vulnerable and open with each other, deepening their emotional connection.

The dynamic between Aries and Scorpio is powerful. Aries' boldness and confidence inspire Scorpio to embrace their own power and take risks. In turn, Scorpio's intensity and emotional depth help ground Aries and encourage them to explore their emotions more deeply. This push-pull dynamic leads to growth, both individually and as a couple.

Their physical connection is equally intense, with a sexual chemistry that is off the charts. Aries and Scorpio share a natural compatibility in their desires, leading to passionate encounters that are not only deeply satisfying but also strengthen their emotional bond. These intimate moments are filled with passion and intensity, deepening their connection in ways that go beyond the physical.

Scorpio's transformative nature has a profound impact on Aries' personal growth. Through their relationship, Scorpio encourages Aries to explore their emotions, confront their vulnerabilities, and embrace emotional healing. Aries, on the other hand, helps Scorpio find healthy outlets for their intense emotions and teaches them to embrace optimism and lightness.

Although their communication styles differ, with Aries being more straightforward and Scorpio more intuitive, both signs value direct and honest communication. Patience and understanding are essential to bridging their differences, and by cultivating these qualities, they can develop a deep level of trust and openness.

Aries and Scorpio also share a fascination with the shadowy and mysterious aspects of life. They are comfortable exploring the depths of the human psyche, creating a safe space for each other to share secrets and vulnerabilities. This mutual understanding allows them to accept each other's complexities and navigate through darkness together.

This relationship offers the potential for profound personal growth and transformation. Aries and Scorpio push each other to confront their fears, break through barriers, and reach their highest potential. Their connection becomes a catalyst for self-discovery, leading to both personal and spiritual growth. In the end, their relationship is built on intense chemistry, emotional depth, and a shared determination to grow together, creating a love that can withstand the tests of time.

Chapter Thirty-Eight

Compatibility Between Aries and Sagittarius

The compatibility between Aries and Sagittarius is an exciting and adventurous combination, fueled by shared enthusiasm and expansive energy. Both signs are driven by a passion for life, and their zest for thrilling experiences makes them natural companions on a quest for adventure. They are drawn to each other's boundless energy and love for excitement, forming a bond that is vibrant and full of possibilities.

Independence is important to both Aries and Sagittarius, and they deeply understand each other's need for personal space and the freedom to pursue individual interests. This shared respect for autonomy allows them to support each other's growth and encourage their separate aspirations, strengthening their connection while maintaining their individuality.

Adventure and exploration are at the core of their relationship. Both are eager to push boundaries, travel, and seek new experiences. Together, they create a whirlwind of energy that keeps their connection dynamic and fresh, constantly finding new ways to enjoy life. Their love for exploration makes them the perfect partners for embarking on thrilling activities and discovering the world together.

Intellectually, Aries and Sagittarius are equally curious, enjoying deep conversations and philosophical discussions. They are both passionate about expanding their knowledge and broadening their understanding of the world. This intellectual connection stimulates their minds and allows them to explore a wide range of topics, adding depth to their bond.

Their natural optimism and positive outlook on life make them a perfect match. They share an infectious enthusiasm that uplifts each other and those around them, creating a joyful and supportive atmosphere in their relationship. This positivity enhances their connection and helps them tackle challenges with a sense of hope and excitement.

Aries and Sagittarius are both direct and outspoken, valuing honest and open communication. They have no reservations about expressing their opinions and desires, which leads to a relationship built on trust and mutual understanding. This transparency allows them to navigate their connection with clarity, ensuring they are always on the same page.

They also inspire each other's personal growth. Aries encourages Sagittarius to be more assertive and decisive, while Sagittarius helps Aries adopt a more expansive, open-minded perspective. Their dynamic pushes each other to grow beyond their comfort zones, enriching their lives both individually and together.

Their shared sense of humor adds another layer to their bond. Aries and Sagittarius are playful and enjoy making each other laugh. Their light-hearted approach to life brings them closer, and their ability to find humor in life's ups and downs strengthens the friendship at the heart of their relationship.

When conflicts arise, Aries and Sagittarius face them head-on with a direct and honest attitude. They address issues openly, appreciating clear communication and practical solutions. This straightforward approach allows them to resolve disagreements quickly and move forward without holding grudges.

At the heart of their relationship is an understanding of the importance of personal freedom. Both Aries and Sagittarius encourage each other to pursue individual passions and explore their own paths, and their relationship thrives because of this shared belief in the power of independence within a partnership.

In summary, Aries and Sagittarius are a perfect match, marked by a shared love for life, adventure, and freedom. Their compatibility is rooted in enthusiasm, intellectual curiosity, and a deep respect for each other's individuality. Together, they embark on a thrilling journey, embracing the world with energy and open hearts.

Chapter Thirty-Nine

Compatibility Between Aries and Capricorn

Aries and Capricorn may seem to be an unlikely pair due to their contrasting personalities, but beneath the surface, they have the potential to form a balanced and complementary relationship. Both signs are driven by ambition and a desire to succeed, though they approach these goals differently. Aries is known for their boldness and natural leadership skills, while Capricorn brings practicality, discipline, and a strong work ethic to the table. Together, they can combine these strengths to form a powerful partnership, with Aries' determination and Capricorn's ability to strategize for the long term.

There is a deep mutual respect between them. Aries admires Capricorn's grounded and focused nature, especially in the face of challenges, while Capricorn respects Aries' courage, assertiveness, and willingness to take risks. This respect creates a solid foundation for their relationship, allowing them to appreciate each other's unique qualities.

The balance between their energies is striking. Aries' passionate and impulsive nature finds stability in Capricorn's more practical, grounded approach. Capricorn's calm demeanor helps temper Aries' enthusiasm, offering a sense of grounding. In return, Aries injects excitement and spontaneity into Capricorn's life, encouraging them to embrace a more adventurous side.

Their shared values also play a big part in their connection. Both value hard work, integrity, and personal growth. These common values create an understanding and alignment, enabling them to work well together toward common goals.

The skills they bring to the table are complementary as well. Aries excels at taking initiative and taking risks, while Capricorn thrives at planning, organizing, and executing tasks with precision. This partnership allows them to use their individual strengths to achieve remarkable outcomes, with Aries pushing forward and Capricorn ensuring everything stays on track.

Capricorn's reliable, grounded nature offers a stable foundation for Aries' ambitions. Capricorn provides steady support and practical advice, helping Aries achieve their goals. On the other hand, Aries brings excitement and inspiration to Capricorn's life, encouraging them to step out of their comfort zone and pursue their dreams.

Both understand the importance of balancing work with leisure. While they are deeply committed to their careers and ambitions, they also recognize the need for rest and enjoyment. By establishing a healthy work-life balance, they are able to relax and have fun while still appreciating the rewards of their hard work.

Though their communication styles may differ—Aries being direct and assertive, while Capricorn tends to be more reserved and cautious—they both value honesty and openness. By listening to each other's viewpoints and being willing to find common ground, they can navigate these differences and create effective compromises.

Capricorn's stability and practicality provide a grounding influence on Aries' emotional intensity. Capricorn offers a calm, nurturing presence, allowing Aries to express their emotions freely. Aries, in turn, helps Capricorn embrace their feelings and loosen up, injecting joy and spontaneity into the relationship.

Both Aries and Capricorn are committed and loyal partners who value long-term relationships. Their shared goals, mutual support, and dedication to overcoming challenges give them the foundation needed to build a lasting partnership. Through understanding, respect, and the willingness to harmonize their different energies, they have the ability to create a partnership that not only supports their individual growth but also allows them to accomplish their collective goals together.

Chapter Forty

Compatibility Between Aries and Aquarius

The connection between Aries and Aquarius is a dynamic blend of passion and intellectual stimulation, with both signs offering something unique that fosters an exciting relationship. Aries brings a boldness and determination, while Aquarius adds an eccentric and unconventional twist, creating a spark of creativity that fuels their partnership. This innovative energy propels them toward new ideas and thrilling ventures, making their time together lively and inspiring.

Both Aries and Aquarius possess sharp intellects and a strong curiosity. They enjoy deep, stimulating conversations and are always seeking to explore new concepts. Aries' direct and spontaneous approach complements Aquarius' abstract and visionary thinking, forming a powerful synergy that keeps their interactions engaging and thought-provoking.

At the core of their relationship, both value their individuality and independence. They understand and respect each other's need for personal space to pursue their own interests, which allows them to maintain a strong connection while still nurturing their individual growth. This mutual respect for freedom is a key part of what makes their relationship work so well.

Aries and Aquarius also share a similar vision for the future. Both idealistic, they desire to make a positive impact on the world, and this shared ambition helps them find common ground. With their aligned goals and aspirations, they can work together harmoniously toward a greater purpose, supporting each other as they strive for meaningful achievements.

Neither Aries nor Aquarius is afraid to challenge the status quo. They both have a rebellious streak and enjoy breaking the mold. This mutual appreciation for each other's uniqueness creates a relationship that celebrates individuality and embraces change. Together, they cultivate an unconventional partnership that thrives on growth, freedom, and exploration.

In their relationship, Aries and Aquarius are strong supporters of one another. Aries' enthusiasm and passion can inspire

Aquarius to chase their dreams, while Aquarius' open-mindedness provides a safe space for Aries to explore new ideas. This mutual encouragement nurtures both individuals' personal growth, allowing each to fully embrace their own paths while staying connected.

While known for their intellectual bond, Aries and Aquarius can also form a deep emotional connection. Aquarius' rational approach to emotions offers Aries clarity and insight, helping them understand their feelings. In return, Aries brings warmth and passion to Aquarius, whose sometimes detached demeanor can be softened by Aries' heartfelt energy. This balance creates a well-rounded emotional connection that complements their intellectual compatibility.

Adventure and excitement are essential to both Aries and Aquarius. They share a love for spontaneity and trying new things, fueling their need for constant exploration and growth. Their shared sense of adventure ensures their lives are filled with exhilarating experiences and a constant push toward new horizons.

Though their communication styles differ—Aries being direct and assertive, while Aquarius takes a more detached and analytical approach—they both value honesty and openness. With mutual respect and a willingness to understand each other's perspectives, they can bridge any communication gaps and collaborate effectively. This ability to communicate openly is a crucial aspect of their relationship.

One of the most significant strengths of their partnership is their acceptance of each other's quirks and eccentricities. Aries and Aquarius both value authenticity, encouraging each other to embrace their true selves without judgment. This unconditional acceptance creates a strong foundation of trust, allowing their relationship to thrive in an environment of openness and understanding.

Ultimately, the compatibility between Aries and Aquarius blends passion, intellectual stimulation, and a shared vision for the future. Their independent spirits, mutual support, and celebration of individuality create a relationship that is filled with adventure, innovation, and personal growth. Together, they form a partnership that is as inspiring as it is exciting.

Chapter Forty-One

Compatibility Between Aries and Pisces

The relationship between Aries and Pisces is a captivating mix of contrasting elements, where fire meets water to create a dynamic and complex connection. At first glance, their differences might seem like a challenge, yet these very contrasts allow them to complement each other in meaningful ways.

Both Aries and Pisces are deeply emotional, though they express their feelings in different ways. Aries is known for their passionate and assertive nature, while Pisces tends to be more sensitive, intuitive, and empathetic. Despite these differences, their emotional depth enables them to connect on a profound level, forming a bond based on understanding and compassion.

Their contrasting strengths further enhance their compatibility. Aries brings a strong sense of direction, assertiveness, and a desire for action, while Pisces offers gentleness, compassion, and a nurturing spirit. These qualities balance each other well, with Aries providing motivation and clarity, and Pisces offering emotional support and understanding when needed.

On a spiritual level, both signs have a deep connection to higher truths. Aries' pioneering nature aligns with Pisces' intuitive abilities, creating a shared interest in exploring spiritual realms. Together, they inspire each other's growth, embarking on a journey that enriches their spiritual understanding.

Creativity flows freely between Aries and Pisces, as both signs possess a rich imaginative outlook on life. Aries brings a bold and innovative approach, while Pisces contributes a dreamy, intuitive perspective. This combination fosters a creative partnership where they can work on projects, artistic endeavors, and shared dreams, making their life together one filled with inspiration and imaginative energy.

In their relationship, Pisces provides a safe and nurturing environment for Aries, offering support and compassion without stifling their need for independence. Aries, in return, can inspire Pisces to pursue their own dreams, encouraging them to take bold steps and find the confidence to move forward in life. This mutual support creates a solid foundation of trust and understanding.

Both signs are adventurous at heart, although their types of adventures differ. Aries seeks external exploration, diving into new experiences, while Pisces enjoys exploring the depths of their imagination and emotions. Together, they embark on journeys that broaden their horizons, be it physical or emotional. Their shared love of adventure helps them grow as individuals and as a couple, with Aries pushing them to take risks while Pisces brings a thoughtful, introspective balance.

Communication between Aries and Pisces can sometimes be challenging due to their different styles. Aries is direct and straightforward, while Pisces tends to be more gentle and indirect. Yet, both value honesty and openness, and with patience and understanding, they can overcome these differences. Through active listening and empathy, they learn to bridge any gaps in communication and develop a deeper understanding of each other's needs.

The relationship between Aries and Pisces thrives on balance. Aries' impulsive and sometimes fiery nature is softened by Pisces' calm and intuitive presence. Pisces helps Aries to pause and consider the emotional consequences of their actions, while Aries brings excitement and encourages Pisces to assert themselves more confidently.

At the core of their connection, Aries and Pisces share a deep sense of compassion for others. Both value kindness and the importance of helping those in need. Their shared empathy leads them to support each other's efforts to make a positive difference in the world, working together to create a meaningful impact.

In the end, the compatibility between Aries and Pisces is a harmonious blend of passion, emotional depth, creativity, and spirituality. Through understanding and acceptance of their differences, they can build a relationship that nurtures both individual growth and shared dreams, making their connection truly fulfilling.

Chapter Forty-Two

Birthdate Similarities

The following "Birthdate" chapters have many similarities and the reason for this is that they are all under the same star chart. There are only so many ways to reword a paragraph. You will notice that there are some differences the closer a birthdate is to another zodiac sign or star chart. We have not used Life Path Numbers because true Life Path Numbers require a birth year. Instead, we have used symbolic numbers to merge with birthdates.

Chapter Forty-Three

Born on March 21

T hose born on March 21 are marked by the astrological influence of Mars, leaving them with a blend of traits that set them apart. They exhibit a courageous drive, often stepping forward with confidence and determination to take on new challenges. Their adventurous spirit is evident, always eager to explore uncharted territory and embrace fresh experiences. Passionate energy is at the core of their pursuits, sparking enthusiasm for life and motivating them to dive into their interests with vigor.

A strong sense of independence defines their approach to life, allowing them to pursue goals with self-reliance and a desire for autonomy. Optimism comes naturally, as they face obstacles with a positive mindset, confident in their ability to overcome any hurdles they may encounter. Resilience guides them through setbacks, enabling them to recover and persevere even in the most trying circumstances. Their charismatic charm draws people in effortlessly, making them magnetic figures in any setting.

From a numerological perspective, those born on March 21 align with the number 6, a symbol of harmony, balance, and nurturing energy. This influence encourages a deep commitment to fostering relationships, with a tendency to prioritize the well-being and happiness of loved ones. The number 6 also imbues them with a desire to maintain balance in their lives, striving for peace and stability. Their compassionate nature drives them to show kindness and empathy toward others, reinforcing their desire to nurture those around them.

In Tarot, the Lovers card, associated with the number 6, reflects themes of unity, harmony, and the power of choice. This card resonates with the lives of March 21-born individuals, who often find themselves navigating relationships with a focus on harmony and deep connections.

Those born on March 21 embody the essence of compassionate pioneers. Their courage, adventurous energy, and passion make them natural leaders, inspiring others to follow their example. They blaze a trail not just with their determination but with a heart full of empathy and a commitment to creating a better world.

March 21 also holds historical significance, with events such as Otto von Bismarck becoming the Chancellor of the German Empire in 1871, guiding the country through a time of political and social transformation. In 1963, Alcatraz Federal Penitentiary closed its doors after 29 years, marking the end of an era in American history. These events echo the themes of leadership, independence, and new beginnings that align with the traits of those born on this day.

In summary, those born on March 21 are cosmic pioneers, driven by a blend of courage, compassion, and an unrelenting zest for life, making their mark on the world with each step they take.

Chapter Forty-Four

Born on March 22

On March 22, the Aries zodiac sign continues to thrive under the influence of Mars, with those born on this day sharing many of the astrological traits of their Aries counterparts while incorporating distinct qualities into their personalities. These March 22-born individuals exhibit courageous initiative, often taking the first step with determination and resolve. They are driven by a bold vision, setting their sights on their goals and pursuing them with unwavering passion and intensity. The energy they bring to their pursuits fuels not only their own endeavors but also inspires others around them.

An independent spirit runs deep in their character, as they assert their autonomy and confidently carve their own path through life. Optimism is another defining trait, allowing them to face challenges with a positive outlook and a strong belief in their ability to overcome obstacles. Resilience is a core strength, enabling them to rise above adversity and persist in the face of difficulties. Their dynamic enthusiasm makes them both engaging and inspiring, effortlessly drawing others into their orbit.

Numerologically, March 22 aligns with the number 7, a symbol of spirituality, introspection, and inner wisdom. This connection imbues them with heightened spiritual intuition, guiding them on their journey of self-discovery and enlightenment. A deep thirst for knowledge drives them to constantly seek a greater understanding of the world and themselves, and they are often led by their inner voice, trusting their instincts as they navigate life's challenges.

The Tarot card associated with the number 7 is The Chariot, symbolizing determination, willpower, and victory. Themes of inner strength and triumph resonate strongly with those born on March 22, reflecting their ability to overcome obstacles through sheer determination and resolve.

Aries born on March 22 are fearless trailblazers, their courageous initiative, bold vision, and passionate energy enabling them to lead with confidence and inspire those around them to follow in their footsteps. The historical events that share this date further echo these qualities. In 1622, the Jamestown Massacre occurred in the Virginia Colony, a significant moment of conflict, while in 1972, the United States Senate passed the Equal Rights Amendment, a landmark step toward ensuring equality and social justice for all. These events reflect the themes of bravery, leadership, and the pursuit of justice, all of which align with the astrological and numerological influences of March 22.

In summary, those born on March 22 are cosmic pioneers, blazing a trail with their courage, vision, and zest for life, leaving a lasting mark on the world around them.

Chapter Forty-Five

Born on March 23

Born on March 23, those under the Aries sign stand out with the powerful influence of Mars, sharing many of the same traits with fellow Aries while adding their own unique qualities. Known for their bold initiative, they approach every endeavor with confidence and determination, always ready to take action. Driven by a strong sense of vision, they eagerly pursue their dreams with focus and unwavering commitment, bringing an enthusiastic spark to everything they do. Their vibrant energy infuses life with passion, motivating them to go after their goals with intensity.

A fiercely independent nature defines their approach to life, allowing them to carve their own path and navigate challenges with a clear sense of direction. Optimism is a key trait, enabling them to tackle difficulties head-on with the belief that they will overcome any obstacles in their way. Their tenacity and resilience help them bounce back from setbacks, staying persistent through tough times. With magnetic confidence, they naturally attract others, inspiring those around them with their assertiveness and determination.

In numerology, March 23 is associated with the number 8, a symbol of strength, ambition, and material success. Those born on this day often display a powerful presence, commanding attention and respect. They are driven by ambitious pursuits, seeking to achieve success both in their personal and professional lives. The number 8's influence leads them to focus on creating financial stability and reaching tangible goals, with a strong desire to leave a lasting impact.

The Tarot card connected to the number 8 is Strength, representing inner strength, courage, and determination. Themes of resilience and personal power align with the path of those born on March 23, reflecting their ability to overcome challenges and assert themselves in the world. As natural leaders, they stand out as ambitious trailblazers, using their visionary drive and tenacious energy to inspire others to reach for greatness.

Historical events that occurred on March 23 also reflect the same themes of leadership, ambition, and resilience. In 1765, the British Parliament passed the Stamp Act, igniting widespread protests and setting the stage for the American Revolution. In 1983, President Ronald Reagan announced the Strategic Defense Initiative, a significant Cold War-era move that underscored the era's tension and ambition.

In summary, those born on March 23 are resilient, ambitious forces who blaze their own path with the strength, confidence, and inner power symbolized by the number 8. Their dynamic presence contributes to the world in meaningful ways, always pushing forward with a sense of purpose and determination.

Chapter Forty-Six

Born on March 24

B orn on March 24, those with the Aries zodiac sign are filled with dynamic energy, influenced by the celestial forces tied to Mars. Sharing the bold and pioneering spirit of Aries, they also embody unique qualities that define their personal journeys. Known for their ability to take bold action, they quickly dive into projects and challenges with courage and determination, never hesitating to get things started. Their creative vision allows them to approach life with fresh ideas, constantly seeking new possibilities and eager to explore innovative avenues.

Passionate drive is at the core of their being, propelling them toward their goals with an enthusiasm and zest for life that can inspire everyone around them. They value their strong-willed independence, confident in their ability to carve their own path.

Even when faced with difficulties, they maintain an optimistic mindset, trusting in their ability to persevere and keep moving forward. Their resilience enables them to bounce back from setbacks, adapting to life's changing circumstances with grace and determination. With their charismatic presence, they naturally draw others toward them, excelling as leaders and influencers in social settings.

The number 9 resonates with those born on March 24, symbolizing wisdom, humanitarianism, and spiritual insight. This number encourages a deep connection to higher ideals, often manifesting as compassion and empathy. People born on this day feel a strong desire to make a positive impact on the world, driven by a sense of responsibility to contribute to the greater good. They tend to approach life with an innate wisdom and profound insight, often seeking to understand the deeper meaning behind life's events. The spiritual connection encouraged by the number 9 leads them to explore their inner world, seeking higher knowledge and understanding.

In Tarot, the card connected to the number 9 is The Hermit, a symbol of introspection, wisdom, and the search for inner truth. Themes of spiritual insight and self-reflection are deeply woven into the lives of those born on March 24, guiding them toward deeper understanding. As compassionate visionaries, they lead with empathy, combining bold action and creative drive with a genuine desire to help others, inspiring those around them to follow their example.

Significant historical events further reflect the themes of leadership, change, and personal transformation linked to this date. In 1603, James VI of Scotland ascended to the English throne, uniting England and Scotland under one monarch, marking a pivotal moment in British history. In 1958, Elvis Presley was inducted into the U.S. Army, a turning point in his career and a cultural milestone of the 1950s.

In summary, those born on March 24 are compassionate, wise leaders, driven by a desire to make a meaningful difference. Guided by the strength and insight of the number 9, they carve their paths with creativity, empathy, and a strong connection to higher ideals, leaving a lasting impact on the world around them.

Chapter Forty-Seven

Born on March 25

Those born on March 25 reflect the bold and proactive nature of Aries, embracing life with confidence and determination. In love and relationships, they are assertive, unafraid to take the lead, and approach their aspirations with the same unwavering commitment. Their enthusiasm is contagious, bringing energy to their endeavors and inspiring those around them to share in their excitement.

They value independence and prefer forging their own path, seeing challenges as opportunities to demonstrate their strength and perseverance. A naturally optimistic outlook allows them to focus on the silver lining, helping them overcome obstacles and stay motivated. Their decisiveness gives them clarity when navigating difficult situations, allowing them to make confident choices and keep moving forward. With a charismatic presence and the ability to inspire others, they are natural leaders, guiding those around them toward shared success.

Numerology connects March 25 to the number 1, a symbol of ambition, innovation, and leadership. Their strong sense of direction and ability to initiate new projects make them well-suited to positions of influence. Intuition plays a vital role in their decision-making, acting as a guiding force that helps them trust their instincts. A constant desire for knowledge fuels their personal growth, combining wisdom and strength in a way that makes them stand out.

In Tarot, the Strength card is linked to this birth date, reflecting courage, resilience, and inner power. These qualities reinforce their ability to lead with vision and determination, inspiring those around them to strive for greatness. With their drive and charisma, they have the potential to accomplish significant achievements both individually and as part of a team.

Significant historical events on March 25 echo themes of leadership and transformation. In 1807, the British Parliament passed the Slave Trade Act, marking a pivotal step toward ending the transatlantic slave trade. In 1957, the Treaty of Rome was signed, laying the foundation for the European Economic Community, which would later evolve into the European Union. In 1998, the Philippines' Department of National Defense and the Armed Forces of the Philippines launched the Balikatan exercise, a joint military initiative with the United States aimed at strengthening defense cooperation.

With bravery, vision, and relentless drive, those born on March 25 have the potential to create their own unique path in life. The stars align in their favor, illuminating a future filled with leadership, inspiration, and achievement.

Chapter Forty-Eight

Born on March 26

Those born on March 26 share the boldness and drive of Aries, embracing life with courage and a strong sense of initiative. At the same time, they have qualities that make them distinct. In relationships, they are unafraid to take the lead, bringing the same level of determination to their personal aspirations. Their energy is infectious, breathing life into everything they do and inspiring those around them to embrace the same enthusiasm.

Independence is deeply valued, and challenges are seen as opportunities to prove resilience and strength. With an optimistic mindset, they approach difficulties with confidence, always seeking the silver lining and staying motivated no matter the circumstances. Decisiveness allows them to navigate complex situations with clarity, ensuring steady progress toward their goals. A natural ability to inspire others often places them in leadership roles, where their charisma and vision guide those around them toward shared success.

Numerology connects March 26 to Master Number 11, a symbol of intuition, inspiration, and enlightenment. This deep sense of insight allows for powerful visionary thinking, helping to guide both personal growth and the ability to uplift others. Intuition is a valuable ally, offering clarity in decision-making and fueling a lifelong journey of self-discovery. A thirst for knowledge drives a constant pursuit of wisdom, blending intellect with inner strength in a way that creates a lasting impact.

In Tarot, the Strength card aligns with this birth date, emphasizing courage, resilience, and unwavering determination. These qualities reinforce a natural ability to lead, offering vision and inspiration to those who follow. With the right mindset and unwavering focus, there is no limit to what can be achieved, especially when working alongside others who share the same drive.

Historical events on March 26 reflect themes of transformation and progress. In 1971, East Pakistan declared its independence, forming the nation of Bangladesh. In 1995, the Schengen Agreement took effect, removing systematic border controls between participating European nations and reshaping the region's approach to travel and cooperation. In 1996, the Philippines hosted the Asia-Pacific Economic Cooperation (APEC) Summit, highlighting its role in regional economic growth and collaboration.

Those born on this day have the potential to stand out in remarkable ways. With bravery, vision, and relentless determination, they can shape their own path and leave a lasting mark on the world. The stars are certainly in their favor.

Chapter Forty-Nine

Born on March 27

Those born on March 27 embody the bold and dynamic nature of Aries, embracing life with courage and determination. While they share the adventurous spirit of their sign, they also have unique qualities that set them apart. In relationships, they approach love with confidence, often taking the lead and pursuing their dreams with unwavering dedication. Their enthusiasm is contagious, bringing energy to every endeavor and inspiring those around them to share in their excitement.

Independence is a defining trait, and they thrive when creating their own path. Challenges are seen as opportunities to prove resilience and demonstrate their strength of will. With a naturally optimistic mindset, they face obstacles with a positive outlook, always finding a way forward. Their decisiveness allows them to navigate complex situations with clarity, ensuring steady progress toward their goals. Charisma and passion for what they do often place them in leadership roles, where they have a talent for motivating and guiding others toward shared success.

Numerology connects March 27 with the number 3, a symbol of creativity, communication, and joy. This influence enhances their ability to express themselves and uplift those around them. Strong intuition serves as a guiding force, offering insight and clarity on their journey of self-discovery and growth. A thirst for knowledge drives them to seek out new ideas and expand their understanding, blending curiosity with inner strength to create a lasting impact.

In Tarot, the Strength card is linked to this birth date, emphasizing courage, resilience, and the power of inner determination. These qualities reinforce a natural ability to lead, inspire, and overcome any challenge. With the right mindset and unwavering focus, there are no limits to what can be achieved, especially when working alongside others who share their drive.

Significant events on March 27 highlight themes of strength and transformation. In 1794, the United States Congress passed the Naval Act, laying the foundation for the U.S. Navy. In 1964, the Great Alaskan Earthquake, the most powerful earthquake in U.S. history, struck Alaska, marking a moment of profound resilience and rebuilding.

Those born on this day have a natural ability to shine in any setting. With their courage, vision, and determination, they have the potential to create a unique and meaningful path in life. The stars are indeed aligned in their favor.

Chapter Fifty

Born on March 28

Those born on March 28 reflect the bold and adventurous nature of Aries, known for facing life with bravery and determination. While they share the energetic spirit of their sign, they also have qualities that make them stand out. In love and in life, they are fearless, often taking the initiative and pursuing their ambitions with relentless dedication. Their enthusiasm is contagious, fueling their pursuits and inspiring those around them to embrace the excitement of new possibilities.

Independence is a defining trait, and they thrive when carving out their own path. Challenges are not obstacles but chances to prove their resilience and determination. With an optimistic mindset, they approach difficulties with confidence, always looking for the bright side and finding ways to move forward. A strong sense of decisiveness allows them to navigate complex situations with clarity, ensuring steady progress toward their goals. Their natural charisma and drive often place them in leadership roles, where they excel at motivating and guiding others toward shared success.

Numerology links March 28 with the number 4, a symbol of stability, practicality, and strong foundations. This influence enhances their ability to build meaningful relationships and create lasting structures in their lives. Intuition serves as a guiding force, providing insight and clarity along their journey of self-discovery. A deep thirst for knowledge fuels their desire to grow, blending curiosity with inner strength to create a powerful presence in any setting.

In Tarot, the Emperor card is connected to this birth date, representing authority, structure, and a strategic mind. These qualities reinforce a natural ability to lead with confidence and vision, inspiring others to work toward shared goals. With focus and determination, there are no limits to what can be achieved, especially when surrounded by a strong and motivated team.

March 28 has seen significant historical events that reflect themes of transformation and influence. In 1849, the United Kingdom formally annexed the Punjab region of India, shaping its history. In 1930, the Turkish government officially renamed Constantinople and Angora as Istanbul and Ankara, marking a major shift in identity. In 1979, the Three Mile Island nuclear accident in Pennsylvania became the most serious incident in the history of American commercial nuclear power, highlighting the importance of resilience and learning from challenges.

Those born on this day have a unique ability to stand out in any crowd. With courage, vision, and unwavering determination, they have the potential to forge their own path in life. The stars are certainly aligned in their favor.

Chapter Fifty-One

Born on March 29

Those born on March 29 are known for their courage, determination, and infectious enthusiasm. They face life with boldness, taking the initiative in both love and ambition. Their energy is uplifting, inspiring those around them to embrace challenges with excitement and confidence. Independence is a defining trait, and they thrive when forging their own path. Obstacles are seen as opportunities to grow stronger, reinforcing their unwavering resolve.

A natural sense of optimism helps them navigate life's ups and downs, always focusing on possibilities rather than limitations. They make decisions with clarity and confidence, allowing them to move forward without hesitation. Their charisma and enthusiasm often place them in leadership roles, where they guide and motivate others toward shared goals.

Numerology connects March 29 to the number 5, symbolizing change, freedom, and adventure. This influence fuels a love for new experiences and an eagerness to explore different ideas. Strong intuition acts as a guiding force, providing insight and clarity in times of uncertainty. A passion for learning drives them to expand their understanding, blending curiosity with inner strength to leave a lasting impact.

In Tarot, the Hierophant card represents this birth date, embodying wisdom, tradition, and spiritual guidance. These qualities add depth to their leadership, allowing them to inspire others with knowledge and vision. With their drive and passion, they have the ability to achieve great things, both independently and as part of a team.

Throughout history, March 29 has been marked by significant events that reflect themes of progress and discovery. In 1849, the United Kingdom formally annexed the Punjab region of India, shaping its future. In 1936, construction of the Hoover Dam began in Nevada, a monumental feat of engineering. In 1974, Mariner 10 became the first spacecraft to pass by Mercury, sending back the first close-up images of the planet and expanding humanity's understanding of the solar system.

With a spirit that shines brightly, those born on this day have the power to shape their own destiny. Their courage, vision, and resilience set them apart, ensuring that they leave a meaningful mark on the world.

Chapter Fifty-Two

Born on March 30

People born on March 30 radiate energy, confidence, and a strong sense of independence. They stand out for their dynamic nature, embracing challenges with enthusiasm and a natural ability to take the lead. With an assertive presence and a bold approach to life, they inspire those around them through their courage and determination.

One of their most defining traits is their remarkable drive. Ambition fuels their actions, pushing them to reach their goals with unwavering perseverance. Obstacles only serve as stepping stones, and they thrive in environments that require initiative and a pioneering spirit. Their willingness to take risks and explore new opportunities keeps them engaged and motivated.

A love for adventure and exploration also shapes their personality. They are drawn to new experiences and are always in search of excitement, whether through travel, learning, or personal challenges. They are not ones to shy away from the unknown, embracing change with open arms and an eagerness to grow.

There is also an undeniable charm to those born on this date. Their magnetic energy naturally attracts people, making them well-liked in social circles. With strong communication skills, they express themselves with confidence and warmth, often serving as motivators and influencers. Their ability to connect with others helps them build meaningful relationships, and their enthusiasm is contagious.

At times, impulsiveness can lead them to act quickly without considering the full consequences of their decisions. While this boldness often serves them well, learning to balance instinct with patience can lead to even greater success. Taking a moment to reflect before making major choices allows them to harness their natural decisiveness more effectively.

In relationships, they bring passion and devotion. Independence remains important to them, so they seek partners who respect their need for personal space while also engaging them in intellectually stimulating conversations. They flourish in relationships that encourage growth and mutual support, where both individuals inspire each other to achieve their aspirations.

Numerology adds another layer of insight into the March 30 personality. By breaking down the numbers, their symbolic number is 6, representing harmony, responsibility, and compassion. While they embody the assertive nature of Aries, the influence of 6 brings a nurturing side, making them both strong and deeply caring. They balance their leadership qualities with a genuine concern for the well-being of those around them, making them not just inspiring figures but also dependable and supportive friends, family members, and partners.

The Tarot card associated with March 30 is The Lovers, a symbol of relationships, choices, and balance. This card highlights their deep emotional connections and their ability to create harmony in their personal and professional lives. It also suggests that they may encounter significant crossroads where decisions must align with their values and desires.

Throughout history, March 30 has been marked by important events that reflect the pioneering and impactful nature of those born on this day. In 1842, anesthesia was first used in surgery, revolutionizing medical procedures. In 1964, the launch of Mariner 4 set the stage for humanity's first close-up images of Mars, showcasing the spirit of exploration. The discovery of the Terracotta Army in 1974 revealed a magnificent piece of ancient history, reminding the world of the lasting influence of great visionaries.

With their natural confidence, adventurous spirit, and compassionate heart, those born on March 30 leave a lasting impression wherever they go. Their ability to lead, connect, and inspire ensures that they make a meaningful impact on the world around them.

Chapter Fifty-Three

Born on March 31

Those born on March 31 shine with the dynamic qualities of Aries, radiating energy, assertiveness, and a deep sense of independence. Their unique combination of traits makes them natural go-getters, always ready to take charge of their lives and embrace challenges head-on.

In matters of the heart, they approach relationships with a fearless and passionate spirit, often taking the initiative when pursuing love. Their ambitious nature drives them to chase their dreams with unwavering determination, ensuring that they leave a lasting impact in both personal and professional spheres. Their enthusiasm is infectious, bringing excitement to their endeavors and inspiring those around them to share in their optimism.

They have a strong sense of self-sufficiency and prefer to carve their own path rather than follow in someone else's footsteps. Challenges become opportunities to showcase resilience and prove their ability to navigate life's complexities. With a natural inclination toward leadership, they exude confidence and decisiveness, making them well-equipped to handle even the most demanding situations. Their charisma allows them to effortlessly inspire and guide others, leading with a vision that motivates those in their circle.

The symbolic number associated with March 31 is 7, which in numerology represents introspection, wisdom, and a deep connection to the search for truth. This influence grants them an intuitive nature, often guiding them toward meaningful discoveries in both their personal and spiritual journeys. Their thirst for knowledge makes them lifelong learners, always eager to expand their understanding of the world.

In Tarot, the Chariot card is linked to this birthdate, signifying determination, control, and the power to overcome obstacles. Just as the Chariot moves forward with purpose, those born on March 31 harness their inner strength to lead, persist, and triumph over challenges. Their bravery and vision make them exceptional leaders, capable of achieving great success with the support of those who believe in their mission.

Throughout history, March 31 has been marked by significant milestones. In 1889, the Eiffel Tower was officially opened to the public, standing as a symbol of architectural brilliance and innovation. In 1966, the Soviet Union launched Luna 10, the first spacecraft to orbit the moon, pushing the boundaries of space exploration. In 1991, the Warsaw Pact was dissolved, bringing an end to a major political and military alliance and reshaping global dynamics.

While those born on this date may sometimes act on impulse, the influence of the number 7 encourages them to pause, reflect, and seek deeper meaning in their decisions. They are willing to invest in creating balanced and meaningful connections with others, ensuring that their relationships are built on understanding and mutual respect.

Chapter Fifty-Four

Born on April 1

Those born on April 1 embody the dynamic essence of Aries, known for their energy, assertiveness, and strong sense of independence. Their distinct combination of traits makes them natural trailblazers, eager to take on new challenges and carve out their own path in life.

In love and relationships, they approach matters of the heart with courage, often taking the lead in expressing their feelings and pursuing meaningful connections. Their ambitious drive pushes them to chase their goals with unwavering determination, ensuring they leave a lasting impression on the world around them. Their enthusiasm is boundless, bringing excitement to their pursuits and inspiring those in their circle to share in their passion.

Independence is deeply important to them, and they thrive when given the freedom to make their own choices. Obstacles are seen as opportunities to prove their resilience and demonstrate their ability to navigate life's twists and turns. With a confident and decisive nature, they handle complex situations with ease, always moving forward with clarity and purpose. Leadership comes naturally, as their charisma and energy make them a source of motivation for those who look to them for guidance.

The symbolic number associated with April 1 is 5, representing adaptability, adventure, and freedom. This influence fuels a deep curiosity and a love for exploration, driving them to seek out new experiences and embrace change. Their adventurous spirit thrives in dynamic environments, where they can continuously learn and grow.

In Tarot, the Fool card is linked to this birthdate, symbolizing spontaneity, innocence, and the courage to take risks. Much like the essence of this card, they approach life with an open heart and a willingness to embark on new journeys, trusting that each step forward will bring fresh opportunities. Their bold vision and fearless nature make them natural explorers, inspiring those around them to embrace the unknown.

History has marked April 1 with significant milestones. In 1976, Apple Inc. was founded by Steve Jobs, Steve Wozniak, and Ronald Wayne, forever changing the landscape of technology. In 2001, the Netherlands became the first country to legalize same-sex marriage, setting a precedent for LGBTQ+ rights worldwide. In 1924, Adolf Hitler was sentenced to five years in prison for his role in the Beer Hall Putsch, though he served only nine months, an event that shaped the course of history.

Aries born on this day may sometimes act on impulse, but the influence of the number 5 encourages them to embrace adventure and remain open to change. They are willing to invest in creating balanced and meaningful relationships, ensuring their connections with others are built on mutual respect and shared experiences.

Chapter Fifty-Five

Born on April 2

T hose born on April 2 reflect the dynamic qualities of Aries, marked by energy, determination, and an independent spirit. Their unique blend of traits makes them both strong-willed and compassionate, with a natural ability to lead and inspire.

In love and relationships, they embrace a fearless approach, often taking the initiative in expressing their feelings. Ambition drives them to pursue their goals with unwavering dedication, ensuring that they make a lasting impact in both their personal and professional lives. Their enthusiasm is infectious, filling their surroundings with a sense of excitement and motivating those around them to share in their passion.

They value independence and prefer to forge their own path, seeing challenges as opportunities to prove their resilience. With a keen ability to stay optimistic, they find silver linings in difficult situations and use that positivity to keep pushing forward. Their sharp decision-making skills and strong sense of confidence allow them to navigate complex situations with ease, always maintaining a clear vision for the future. Leadership comes naturally, as their charisma and energy make them a guiding force for those who seek direction.

April 2 is associated with the number 6 in numerology, symbolizing love, nurturing, and family. This influence encourages them to cultivate deep and meaningful relationships, placing great importance on harmony and emotional connection. Their caring nature makes them a source of support for their loved ones, and they find fulfillment in strengthening family bonds and maintaining a sense of unity at home.

The Lovers card in Tarot is linked to this birthdate, representing love, unity, and important choices in relationships. They have an innate desire to nurture, providing love and support to those they cherish. Their ability to bring people together and foster connection highlights their deep sense of devotion.

History has marked April 2 with significant events. In 1972, Sesame Street made its television debut, becoming an iconic source of education and entertainment for children worldwide. In 1805, the United States Military Academy at West Point was established, growing into one of the most prestigious military institutions. In 2005, Pope John Paul II passed away at the age of 84, concluding over 26 years of leadership as the head of the Catholic Church.

Born on this day, Aries natives embody both strength and warmth. Their leadership, compassion, and unwavering optimism set them apart, making them natural caregivers and inspiring figures in the lives of those around them. Maintaining harmony in relationships is a priority, and they consistently strive to uplift and support those they love.

Chapter Fifty-Six

Born on April 3

Born under the sign of Aries, those who celebrate their birthday on April 3 inherit qualities of assertiveness, courage, and independence. Their presence is magnetic, filled with an energy that inspires and captivates those around them. Naturally inclined to take charge, they step into leadership roles with confidence and determination, making their mark wherever they go.

Their drive to achieve is a defining trait, pushing them to turn their ambitions into reality. Challenges are not seen as roadblocks but as opportunities to grow, and setbacks only fuel their perseverance. With resilience at their core, they navigate life's ups and downs with a mindset focused on progress and self-improvement. A thirst for adventure keeps them constantly seeking new experiences, unafraid of stepping into the unknown. They embrace change with open arms, always eager to expand their understanding and push their own boundaries.

With a charm that effortlessly draws people in, they build strong connections and thrive in social settings. Communication comes naturally, and their enthusiasm makes them engaging speakers who can motivate and uplift those around them. Their ability to lead is strengthened by their charisma, allowing them to influence and inspire in meaningful ways.

At times, their passionate nature can lead to impulsive decisions. Quick to act, they may not always fully consider the consequences, making self-awareness an important skill to develop. Learning patience and practicing mindfulness can help them find a balance between spontaneity and careful thought, leading to wiser choices in both personal and professional matters.

In relationships, they are passionate and devoted, valuing both connection and independence. A strong partnership for them is one that fosters mutual growth and respects personal freedom. Their loyalty runs deep, and they thrive in relationships that encourage both love and individual aspirations. They seek intellectual stimulation in their connections, always looking for ways to inspire and support their partner.

Numerology reveals deeper insights into the nature of those born on April 3. Adding the digits of the date, 4 (April) + 3, results in the number 7, which carries a highly spiritual and introspective energy. This influence gives them a deep connection to their inner world and a strong desire for knowledge and understanding. They are naturally drawn to philosophical and metaphysical subjects, always searching for deeper truths. With an analytical mind, they excel in areas that require deep thought, research, and uncovering hidden meanings. Solitude is important to them, providing the space to reflect and grow. Practices like meditation, mindfulness, and self-exploration often appeal to them, allowing them to gain clarity and insight into their emotions and thoughts.

April 3 has also seen significant moments in history. In 33 AD, Christian tradition marks this as the date of the crucifixion of Jesus Christ. In 1043, Edward the Confessor was crowned King of England. In 1973, Martin Cooper, a Motorola employee, made the first handheld mobile phone call in New York City, changing the course of communication forever.

Balancing their adventurous spirit with moments of reflection, those born on April 3 embody both strength and wisdom. Their ability to lead, inspire, and seek deeper understanding sets them apart, making them both powerful forces of change and thoughtful seekers of truth.

Chapter Fifty-Seven

Born on April 4

Those born on April 4th are Aries, the first sign of the zodiac, which brings a bold and energetic personality. Confidence, courage, and independence shape their character, making them natural leaders who inspire others with enthusiasm and a take-charge attitude.

A deep sense of determination defines their approach to life. Setting ambitious goals comes naturally, and challenges only fuel their drive. Rather than being discouraged by setbacks, they use them as stepping stones, growing stronger with each obstacle they overcome. Their adventurous spirit thrives on new experiences, and change excites them rather than intimidates them. Pushing past comfort zones is second nature, and curiosity keeps them constantly learning and evolving.

People are naturally drawn to their charisma and outgoing nature. They form connections easily, making friends across different circles. With strong communication skills and confidence, they have a way of influencing and motivating those around them. Their passion, while admirable, sometimes leads to impulsive decisions. Taking a step back to reflect before acting can help create a more balanced approach, and patience will serve them well on their journey.

In relationships, passion and devotion define their love life, yet personal freedom remains important. A partner who respects their independence and supports their ambitions is essential. The ideal relationship is one filled with intellectual stimulation and mutual growth, where both partners thrive as individuals and together.

April 4th is also connected to the symbolic number 8 in numerology, reinforcing their natural ambition and leadership qualities. This number is often linked to power and success, strengthening their drive to achieve. It also represents balance and responsibility, instilling a deep understanding of ethics and accountability. While Aries energy may sometimes lead to impulsive moments, the influence of the number 8 encourages a more strategic and calculated approach to achieving goals.

Throughout history, April 4th has been marked by significant events. In 1581, Francis Drake completed his circumnavigation of the world, becoming the first Englishman to do so. In 1818, the United States Congress adopted a new flag design, featuring 13 red and white stripes and one star for each of the 20 states at the time. In 1949, twelve nations came together to sign the North Atlantic Treaty, forming NATO as a key alliance during the Cold War.

In conclusion, those born on this day are known for their bold and ambitious nature, paired with a keen sense of balance and responsibility. Their determination and strong ethical foundation position them for success in life, allowing them to achieve great things while making a meaningful impact on the world around them.

Chapter Fifty-Eight

Born on April 5

Those born on April 5th fall under the sign of Aries, the first in the zodiac. This brings a bold and passionate nature, along with a strong sense of independence, courage, and an innate love for exploration. Energy and enthusiasm come naturally, making them a source of inspiration for those around them. Leadership often feels like second nature, as they have a way of stepping up and taking charge in any situation.

Determination is a defining trait, driving them to set ambitious goals and pursue them with relentless passion. Challenges are met head-on, and setbacks serve as valuable lessons rather than roadblocks. Each obstacle only adds to their strength, reinforcing their ability to push forward and achieve even greater success.

A deep sense of adventure keeps life exciting. The thrill of new experiences is irresistible, and change is welcomed rather than feared. Curiosity fuels a constant desire to learn and grow, ensuring that life is never stagnant. Whether through travel, intellectual pursuits, or personal challenges, they seek out opportunities to expand their horizons.

People are naturally drawn to their charisma and enthusiasm. Their social and outgoing nature makes it easy to connect with a wide range of personalities, and strong communication skills allow them to inspire and motivate others effortlessly. Confidence and optimism make them natural influencers, always pushing those around them toward greater possibilities.

At times, their passionate approach to life can lead to impulsive decisions. Taking a moment to reflect before acting helps create a more balanced perspective. Patience and mindfulness serve as valuable tools that enhance their ability to make thoughtful choices while maintaining their adventurous spirit.

In relationships, deep passion and devotion define their love life, yet maintaining personal freedom is just as important. A partner who respects their independence and encourages personal growth is essential. The best connections come from relationships that stimulate the mind and allow both people to thrive as a team while continuing to grow individually.

April 5th also carries the influence of the number 9 in numerology, which brings a strong sense of compassion and a deep-rooted desire to make a positive impact. Leadership is not just about ambition but also about service and empathy. This combination creates a leader who is both strong and caring, someone who inspires others while genuinely looking out for their well-being.

The influence of the number 9 creates a natural inclination to help others, making fulfillment more likely when involved in work that benefits the community. Whether through social work, advocacy, or humanitarian efforts, they are drawn to causes that create meaningful change. The number 9 is also connected to transformation, meaning life will be filled with moments of personal growth that shape them into an even more compassionate and understanding person.

While Aries energy may sometimes bring impulsiveness, the presence of the number 9 encourages thoughtfulness. Leadership is not just about taking charge but also about fostering a supportive environment where others can thrive.

April 5th is a day marked by significant historical events. In 1614, Pocahontas married John Rolfe, a union that brought a temporary period of peace between English settlers and the Powhatan people. In 1792, George Washington exercised the first presidential veto in U.S. history, demonstrating the power of checks and balances in government. In 1992, the Bosnian

War began, leading to one of the longest and most devastating sieges in modern history.

Those born on this day embody both strength and compassion, blending ambition with a deep sense of responsibility toward others. Their determination and ability to inspire make them well-equipped to achieve greatness while making a meaningful difference in the world.

Chapter Fifty-Nine

Born on April 6

As an Aries, you're a true trailblazer, always ready to take on new challenges with enthusiasm and a strong sense of purpose. Passion and determination define your approach to life, pushing you to forge your own path and inspire those around you. Independence comes naturally, and you thrive when you're leading the charge toward exciting new opportunities.

Your ability to set ambitious goals and tackle them head-on is one of your strongest qualities. Obstacles don't deter you—they fuel your persistence, making you more determined than ever to succeed. Every setback is just another step toward something greater, and your resilience ensures that nothing holds you back for long.

Adventure calls to you, and you're always eager to embrace change. Whether it's exploring new places, trying different experiences, or pushing the boundaries of what's possible, you're at your best when life is full of movement and discovery. A natural curiosity drives you to expand your knowledge and seek out new horizons, ensuring that there's never a dull moment in your world.

People are naturally drawn to your confidence and charm. You have a gift for making connections, forming friendships easily with a wide range of people. Your strong communication skills and ability to inspire make you a natural motivator, encouraging others to embrace their own ambitions and dreams.

Your passion can sometimes lead to impulsive decisions, but taking a moment to pause and reflect can help you make more thoughtful choices. Learning patience and mindfulness will serve you well as you continue on your journey, ensuring that your energy is channeled in the most effective ways.

In love, you bring intensity and devotion, but you also value your freedom. A partner who understands and respects your need for independence will be the perfect match—someone who can challenge you intellectually while supporting your personal growth. Relationships thrive when both partners can evolve together, creating a dynamic and exciting bond.

April 6th carries the influence of the number 1 in numerology, a number associated with leadership, ambition, and fresh starts. This adds an extra layer of confidence and drive, reinforcing your ability to take initiative and carve out your own success. You have a unique vision and a strong desire to make a meaningful impact, always looking ahead to what's next.

This number also highlights the importance of self-discovery and unity. You're deeply in tune with who you are and unafraid to stand out from the crowd. While Aries energy can sometimes be impulsive, the number 1 encourages you to take well-calculated risks, ensuring that your bold moves are backed by focus and strategy.

Looking back at history, April 6th has seen some remarkable moments. In 1917, the United States entered World War I, shifting the course of the conflict with its support. In 1896, the first modern Olympic Games opened in Athens, Greece, reviving an ancient tradition that continues to inspire global competition. And in 1965, the launch of the Early Bird satellite revolutionized global communications, making it possible for people around the world to connect like never before.

Those born on this day are natural leaders, filled with ambition and a pioneering spirit that drives them to push boundaries and achieve great things. With an unstoppable determination and a bold approach to life, they leave a lasting impact wherever they go.

Chapter Sixty

Born on April 7

Being born on April 7 means embracing life with boldness, especially when it comes to relationships and personal aspirations. Love is approached with confidence, as you are unafraid to take the first step in forming meaningful connections. The same fearless attitude extends to your ambitions, where stepping outside your comfort zone feels more like an adventure than a challenge.

Your energy is infectious, igniting enthusiasm not just in yourself but also in those around you. Passion fuels your pursuits, creating momentum in any endeavor you take on. There's a strong desire for independence, and you thrive when given the freedom to forge your own path. Obstacles don't discourage you—they motivate you to push forward and prove your resilience.

Optimism is one of your defining traits. You naturally focus on the bright side, using your positive mindset to overcome difficulties and stay on track toward your goals. Decisiveness is another strength, as you have an instinct for making clear and confident choices, ensuring you're always moving forward, no matter the circumstances.

People are drawn to your charisma and enthusiasm, often looking to you for leadership. Whether intentionally or not, you inspire others, guiding them toward shared goals. Your ability to energize and motivate makes you a powerful presence in any setting.

April 7 is closely linked to the Master Number 11 in numerology, a number associated with heightened intuition, visionary thinking, and deep insight. Those influenced by this number often have an almost uncanny ability to understand underlying truths. There's a natural draw toward inspiring and uplifting others, and an intuitive sense that often leads you in the right direction. It's common for you to "just know" things before they happen, which allows you to navigate difficult situations with clarity. This visionary quality helps you recognize opportunities where others might not, making you a source of inspiration.

Your journey is one of self-discovery, as the Master 11 pushes you toward continual personal growth. Emotional and spiritual understanding play a major role in your development, deepening your insight and bringing you closer to fulfilling your purpose.

The Tarot card associated with April 7 is the High Priestess, a symbol of wisdom, intuition, and inner knowing. Much like this card, you have a deep connection to the unseen and the subconscious, often guided by an inner voice that leads you toward truth and understanding. Many see you as a teacher, someone who naturally helps others explore the deeper aspects of life.

On this day in history, the world saw the establishment of the World Health Organization in 1948, a defining moment in global health. In 1969, the foundation of the internet was laid with the first Request for Comments (RFC) document, forever changing communication. And in 1994, Nelson Mandela was inaugurated as South Africa's first Black president, marking a historic turning point in the fight against apartheid.

The wonderful people born on April 7 shine with courage, boundless energy, and an unstoppable drive for independence. Optimism and decisiveness define their journey, while the influence of the Master Number 11 enhances their intuitive and visionary nature. Paired with the wisdom of the High Priestess, they embody spiritual insight and the power to inspire transformation, both within themselves and in those lucky enough to know them.

Chapter Sixty-One

Born on April 8

Being born on April 8 means embracing the dynamic energy of Aries, a sign known for independence, self-expression, and the courage to take on new adventures. Confidence and charisma propel you forward, making you a natural leader in any new endeavor. Determination is one of your defining qualities. When you set a goal, nothing stands in your way. Challenges only fuel your persistence, and setbacks become stepping stones toward even greater achievements. Strength comes not just from ambition but from the resilience that allows you to emerge stronger after every obstacle.

Bravery is a core part of your nature. You meet difficulties head-on, rarely hesitating or allowing setbacks to slow you down. With a spirit that refuses to be deterred, you push forward, always ready for the next challenge. Creativity flows naturally to you. Fresh experiences excite you, and you're drawn to pushing boundaries and exploring new ideas. This originality makes you a problem solver and a true innovator, carving out your own path rather than following anyone else's.

Passion and adventure shape your approach to relationships. You crave a connection that matches your energy and enthusiasm for life. Romance, for you, is fueled by spontaneity and excitement, with a deep appreciation for those who share your zest for the unexpected. While your drive for instant results can be an asset, it also requires balance. Learning to channel your energy with patience and discipline will bring greater long-term success.

Communication is one of your strongest assets. Whether speaking or writing, you express yourself with confidence and clarity, drawing people in with your natural ability to engage and persuade. This dynamic presence makes you thrive in social settings where you can share ideas and influence those around you. In the professional world, your ambition leads you to roles where you can take charge. Fields that require initiative, leadership, or a competitive edge—such as entrepreneurship, management, or sales—suit you well.

April 8 is also connected to the number 3 in numerology, adding a layer of creativity, self-expression, and social charm to your already dynamic Aries nature. This influence encourages artistic expression, making you naturally inclined toward music, writing, art, or performance. Your assertiveness paired with creativity allows you to stand out in any field you pursue. The number 3 also enhances your social nature. Playful, friendly, and engaging, you thrive in environments that allow you to connect with others and share your enthusiasm for life.

Throughout history, this date has seen remarkable events that reflect the same boldness and impact associated with April 8 birthdays. In 1974, Hank Aaron made history by breaking Babe Ruth's long-standing home run record, demonstrating perseverance and determination in the face of adversity. In 1994, the world lost Kurt Cobain, whose influence on music and culture remains profound. And in 1904, the signing of the Entente Cordiale between the United Kingdom and France marked the end of centuries of conflict and the beginning of a new diplomatic alliance.

With a strong will, an expressive spirit, and the ability to inspire those around you, April 8 is a day that belongs to trailblazers. Whether through leadership, creativity, or connection with others, your influence is undeniable, shaping the world in bold and exciting ways.

Chapter Sixty-Two

Born on April 9

As an Aries born on April 9th, your energy shines through in your passion for independence and new ventures. Confidence and charisma naturally place you in leadership roles, inspiring those around you to follow your example. You take on challenges with determination, setting ambitious goals and pursuing them with relentless focus. Setbacks never deter you; instead, they fuel your resilience, making you stronger with each obstacle you overcome.

Fearlessness and tenacity define your approach to life. You don't back down when faced with difficulties, tackling them head-on with a bold spirit. Your ability to think creatively sets you apart, allowing you to generate innovative ideas and push boundaries. You thrive on new experiences and enjoy finding solutions in ways that others might not consider. This adventurous mindset makes you a natural trailblazer, unafraid to carve your own unique path.

In relationships, passion and excitement are key. You seek a partner who can match your energy and share in life's adventures. Spontaneity is important to you, and you bring enthusiasm into romance, valuing deep connections that keep the spark alive. Your drive for immediate results can sometimes lead to impatience, but learning to balance this with focus and discipline will help you achieve long-term success.

Communication is another one of your strengths. You express your thoughts with confidence and persuasion, making you a powerful presence in social settings. People are drawn to your dynamic personality, and your ability to engage with others allows you to influence and inspire. With your ambitious nature, careers that let you take charge and lead are ideal. Whether in entrepreneurship, management, or fields that require initiative, you thrive in environments where you can make an impact.

April 9th is closely linked to the number 4 in numerology, bringing stability and organization to your naturally driven Aries nature. This number strengthens your ability to stay focused and see projects through to completion. You are not only passionate about starting things but also about finishing them with precision. The combination of your assertiveness and discipline makes you a force to be reckoned with, helping you turn ideas into concrete results. Your reliability and sense of responsibility make you someone others trust, especially in challenging situations.

Throughout history, April 9th has marked significant events that reflect strength and resilience. In 1865, General Robert E. Lee surrendered to General Ulysses S. Grant at Appomattox, bringing an end to the American Civil War. This moment symbolized a turning point in history, leading to the reunification of a divided nation. On the same date in 1942, American and Filipino forces surrendered in the Philippines, leading to the tragic Bataan Death March, a testament to perseverance in the face of hardship. In 1918, Germany launched Operation Michael during World War I, an ambitious attempt to shift the tide of war, demonstrating both strategic planning and intense determination.

Born on this day, you embody the strength, resilience, and leadership that have shaped history. Your ability to balance drive with practicality sets you up for success, allowing you to turn ambition into lasting achievements. The world is waiting for you to bring your bold ideas to life, creating something meaningful with both passion and purpose.

Chapter Sixty-Three

Born on April 10

As an Aries born on April 10th, you shine as a fearless pioneer. Independence drives you, and new adventures excite you. With natural confidence, you step into uncharted territory, eager to take the lead and forge new paths. Ruled by Mars, the planet of action, your energy is boundless, and your determination is unwavering. You charge forward with enthusiasm, inspiring others to embrace challenges with the same bold spirit.

Your passion fuels a life of productivity and creativity. A restless desire for excellence keeps you pushing limits, always seeking the next great challenge. Decisions come quickly, and hesitation is not in your nature. You trust your instincts, act decisively, and thrive when taking charge. While your ability to move swiftly sets you apart, learning to slow down and consider long-term consequences will help you reach even greater heights.

In love, you are loyal and adventurous. Relationships need excitement, spontaneity, and a partner who shares your zest for life. While your strong-willed nature can lead to conflicts, balance is key. Honoring both your independence and the needs of your partner will strengthen your connections.

When it comes to your career, leadership is second nature. Positions that require initiative, risk-taking, and decisive action suit you best. You are drawn to work that allows you to make a lasting impact and achieve meaningful success. Your ability to overcome obstacles makes you a force to be reckoned with in any field.

Numerology adds an extra layer of depth to your personality. The number 5, associated with adaptability, freedom, and curiosity, complements your Aries traits. You embrace change and seek variety, thriving in dynamic environments that require quick thinking. Your adventurous streak leads you toward unconventional paths, where you can explore, create, and redefine success on your own terms. While taking risks excites you, a thoughtful approach helps you turn bold ideas into tangible accomplishments.

April 10th also marks significant moments in history. The Titanic set sail on this day in 1912, embarking on its ill-fated maiden voyage. In 1998, the Good Friday Agreement was signed, bringing peace to Northern Ireland after years of conflict. And in 1949, the Berlin Airlift began winding down, a powerful symbol of resilience in the face of adversity.

Born on this day, you carry a unique blend of courage, ambition, and adaptability. Your ability to lead, explore, and inspire makes you a driving force in any endeavor. The world is full of opportunities, and your spirit is ready to take on whatever comes next.

Chapter Sixty-Four

Born on April 11

As an Aries born on April 11, you carry the fearless energy of the zodiac's trailblazer. A strong sense of independence fuels your drive to take the lead, venture into new territory, and embrace fresh beginnings. Confidence radiates from you, making leadership a natural role as you inspire others with your enthusiasm and determination.

Mars, the planet of action, amplifies your courage and ambition, pushing you to take charge in any situation. You thrive in competitive environments, drawn to challenges that test your resilience. Taking risks doesn't intimidate you—in fact, you seek opportunities to push boundaries and break new ground. The freedom to carve your own path is essential, as you value self-expression and refuse to conform to expectations.

Your sharp intellect and quick perception make you a strong problem solver, and your persuasive communication skills leave a lasting impression. Whether in conversation or in action, your assertiveness commands attention. You set high standards for yourself and refuse to settle for anything less than success, channeling your energy into meaningful pursuits.

In relationships, you bring passion, loyalty, and an adventurous spirit. Excitement in romance keeps you engaged, and you appreciate a partner who matches your energy and curiosity about the world. While your independent nature is a strength, balancing personal freedom with emotional connection is key to maintaining harmony in your relationships.

Although your decisiveness propels you forward, patience isn't always your strongest trait. Learning to pause and consider long-term consequences can help you make even more effective choices, both personally and professionally. With a natural ability to lead, you excel in roles that require initiative, motivation, and vision. Whether in business, sports, or creative endeavors, your presence has a lasting impact.

The influence of the number 6 in numerology adds depth to your Aries nature, bringing a sense of compassion, responsibility, and a desire to support those around you. While you are bold and driven, you also understand the importance of relationships and community. This influence makes you a leader who not only strives for success but also cares about the well-being of others. Whether through mentorship, family connections, or careers centered on helping people, your ability to balance ambition with empathy makes you both powerful and approachable.

Significant historical events have shaped the world on this day. On April 11, 1961, Adolf Eichmann, a key figure in the Holocaust, went on trial in Israel, marking an important moment in the pursuit of justice for war crimes. In 1968, the Civil Rights Act was signed into law, a major milestone in the fight against racial discrimination in housing. And in 1970, Apollo 13 launched, a mission that, despite its unexpected crisis, became a testament to human ingenuity and perseverance.

Born on April 11, you carry the qualities of a strong leader with a compassionate heart. Your boldness allows you to take on challenges with confidence, while your empathy ensures that your influence uplifts those around you. With your adventurous spirit and determination, there's no limit to what you can achieve.

Chapter Sixty-Five

Born on April 12

As an Aries born on April 12th, your presence is bold and unmistakable. Confidence radiates from you, drawing people in with a natural magnetism that sets you apart. Fueled by the energy of Mars, you have an undeniable drive to carve your own path, embracing new challenges and adventures without hesitation. Independence is at the core of who you are, pushing you to seek fresh experiences and forge ahead with determination.

Your enthusiasm is contagious, inspiring those around you with a dynamic and captivating spirit. You communicate with passion, bringing ideas to life with energy and conviction. There is a competitive edge to your nature, and you thrive in environments where you can put your skills to the test. Ambition fuels your every move, and once you set your sights on a goal, you pursue it with relentless focus.

Curiosity and intellect shape the way you navigate the world. A quick thinker with a sharp mind, you enjoy problem-solving and discovering new perspectives. Your ability to analyze situations with clarity makes you a strong decision-maker, while your leadership instincts inspire others to follow your lead. You value honesty and directness, especially in relationships, where you are fiercely loyal and protective. A deep sense of devotion defines the way you love, and you seek partners who can match both your intensity and your sense of adventure.

While your instinct to act quickly often leads to success, learning to temper impulsiveness with patience is key to achieving long-term fulfillment. Taking moments to pause and reflect allows you to align your actions with your broader aspirations. You are drawn to careers that offer autonomy and leadership opportunities, where your natural confidence and determination can shine. Whether in business, management, or other high-energy fields, you excel in positions that challenge and push you forward.

The influence of the number 7 in numerology adds depth to your Aries nature, bringing an introspective quality to your personality. There is a wisdom in your approach that balances your instinct to act with a desire to understand. You are drawn to deeper truths, whether through philosophy, psychology, or spirituality, and your intuition allows you to perceive nuances that others might miss. While Aries thrives on action, this thoughtful energy encourages reflection, helping you find clarity and insight in moments of solitude.

History echoes the bold spirit of April 12th with groundbreaking moments of exploration and transformation. In 1961, Yuri Gagarin became the first human to journey into space, a testament to the daring pursuit of the unknown. One hundred years earlier, in 1861, the first shots of the American Civil War signaled a turning point in history, reshaping the course of a nation. The spirit of discovery continued in 1981 with the launch of the Space Shuttle Columbia, marking a new era in space exploration.

Born on this day, you embody both fearless leadership and thoughtful wisdom. Your ability to take action while seeking deeper understanding sets you apart, allowing you to make an impact while staying true to yourself. The world is yours to conquer, Aries, and with your fire tempered by insight, your path is bound for greatness.

Chapter Sixty-Six

Born on April 13

As an Aries born on April 13th, your presence is bold, dynamic, and impossible to ignore. Confidence radiates from you, a natural force driven by the energy of Mars. Leadership comes effortlessly, and your determination is unwavering. No challenge is too great, and no obstacle too intimidating—you charge forward with a spirit that inspires those around you.

Adventure calls to you, and routine is never enough. A restless energy fuels your desire to seek new experiences, embrace risks, and push beyond limitations. Whether pursuing personal growth or professional ambitions, you thrive when exploring uncharted territory. Your ability to communicate is just as powerful as your drive. Expressing yourself with clarity and conviction, you naturally draw people in, motivating them with your passion and enthusiasm. Competitive environments bring out your best, offering the perfect stage to showcase your skills and prove what you're capable of.

Love is just as intense. Passionate and devoted, you value honesty and loyalty, seeking a partner who can match your energy and share in life's adventures. Protecting those you care about comes naturally, and you'll go to great lengths to ensure their happiness and security. While your impulsive nature keeps life exciting, learning to slow down and think through decisions can help bring long-term success. Patience and self-discipline are essential tools in making sure your ambitions align with the future you envision.

Career paths that allow independence, authority, and innovation are the most fulfilling. Whether as an entrepreneur, a leader in business, or in any field that rewards initiative, you shine when taking charge and inspiring those around you. The influence of the number 8 in numerology adds an extra layer of ambition, success, and responsibility to your character. You recognize the value of perseverance and understand that true achievement comes with accountability. Though you may be driven by immediate goals, there is also an awareness of long-term rewards, and you work toward creating something lasting.

Throughout history, April 13th has marked events that shaped the world. In 1941, Axis forces invaded Yugoslavia and

Greece during World War II, changing the course of the Balkans Campaign. In 1919, the tragic Jallianwala Bagh massacre in Amritsar left an indelible mark on India's history, a reminder of the power struggle between oppression and freedom. More recently, in 1992, the Great Chicago Flood demonstrated how quickly unexpected forces can alter the landscape of a city.

Being born on this date means carrying an incredible blend of bold leadership and an ambition that refuses to be ignored. Success is within reach, and with the right balance of drive and reflection, you can achieve greatness. The world is ready for your energy, Aries—step forward with confidence and make your mark.

Chapter Sixty-Seven

Born on April 14

If you were born on April 14th, you embody the spirit of Aries, the zodiac's bold ram. With the energy of Mars guiding you, confidence and determination flow naturally. Ambitious and driven, you have an innate desire to succeed and lead, making your presence impossible to ignore. You're always looking for ways to leave a lasting impression, and no challenge stands in your way as you pursue your goals with laser focus.

Boldness and fearlessness define you. Independence is at your core, and you constantly strive to achieve greatness. You exude a captivating charm that draws people in, whether you're sharing your ideas or motivating others. With your exceptional communication skills, you articulate your thoughts with clarity and conviction. Your infectious enthusiasm encourages those around you to tap into their own potential and chase their dreams.

Your competitive nature thrives in environments where your talents can be recognized. Leadership positions seem destined for you, as you have a natural ability to inspire and guide others toward success. At the same time, your mind is sharp and quick, always searching for innovative solutions to problems. Your adaptability and strategic thinking make you a valuable asset in any field that requires quick decision-making and planning.

In relationships, you are passionate and fiercely loyal. Honesty, loyalty, and directness are the foundation of your connections. You seek partners who share your energy and commitment to growth, becoming a protector and support system for those you care about. While impulsiveness may sometimes lead to hasty decisions, learning to channel your energy into calculated actions ensures lasting success.

You thrive in careers that allow you to take charge and make a difference. Your leadership is at its best in positions where you can be independent, ambitious, and strategic. Whether you're in entrepreneurship, management, or consulting, any role that demands initiative and drives positive change aligns perfectly with your nature.

The number 9 in numerology adds another layer to your Aries traits. It represents compassion, idealism, and a deep desire to serve others. This influence enhances your leadership with a sense of empathy, balancing your assertiveness with genuine concern for the well-being of those you lead. You may be drawn to careers or causes that allow you to make a positive social impact, whether through charity, volunteer work, or advocacy. The number 9 also signals a period of transformation, suggesting that life changes will help you grow and gain a deeper understanding of yourself and the world around you.

Throughout history, April 14th has witnessed significant events. In 1912, the RMS Titanic tragically sank after striking an iceberg, leading to the deaths of over 1,500 people. In 1865, President Abraham Lincoln was assassinated, a pivotal moment in American history. And in 1935, the "Black Sunday" dust storm swept across the Great Plains, highlighting the environmental devastation of the Dust Bowl.

Born on April 14th, you're a perfect blend of assertiveness and compassion, with an ability to inspire and lead. Your ambition is driven by a desire to make a meaningful impact, and your leadership can inspire others to follow your lead. The world is ready for your energy, Aries, guided by empathy and a passion to create change.

Born on April 15

If you were born on April 15th, you're an Aries, the bold and pioneering ram. You are a dynamic force of nature, full of confidence, passion, and a strong drive to succeed. With Mars guiding you, there's an undeniable sense of ambition within you, pushing you to lead and make a lasting impact on the world.

Courage and independence are your trademarks. You meet challenges with fearlessness, using each one as a stepping stone to further success. Your confidence and determination help you turn obstacles into opportunities, and you face adversity with unshakable tenacity.

Your charisma is magnetic, and it's easy for people to be drawn to you. You lead effortlessly in social situations, and your passion and conviction in communication inspire others to follow your lead. Your enthusiasm is contagious, motivating those around you to push themselves to achieve more.

Driven by a competitive spirit, you're committed to excelling in all areas of life. Your natural leadership shines brightest in environments that require strategic thinking and quick decisions. Whether you're guiding a team, launching new projects, or striving toward personal goals, you're unstoppable in your pursuit of success.

Your intellect is sharp and always eager for new insights. Quick thinking and effective problem-solving come naturally to you, making you a valuable asset in any field requiring adaptability and innovative solutions.

In relationships, your passion and loyalty define you. Honesty and trust are essential to you, and you seek partners who share your ambition and intensity. Once you commit, you protect your loved ones with fierce devotion, ensuring they always feel supported and cherished.

While your bold nature and impulsive tendencies can help propel you forward, it's important to channel your energy with focus to ensure long-term success. Taking the time to reflect before acting will help you make decisions that lead to lasting progress.

You thrive in careers where you can take charge and be in control. Whether it's entrepreneurship, management, politics, or any role where you can drive change and make impactful decisions, you excel in fields that demand ambition, independence, and visionary thinking.

In numerology, the number 1 represents independence, initiative, and leadership, aligning perfectly with your Aries traits. This number amplifies your drive to be a trailblazer, encouraging you to carve your own path and trust in your unique journey. The number 1 strengthens your leadership abilities and enhances your capacity to take risks, inspiring others to follow your lead. It also symbolizes new beginnings, meaning you're often drawn to fresh starts and new ventures, embracing each opportunity with enthusiasm and excitement.

April 15th also holds significance in history. In 1912, the RMS Titanic tragically sank after striking an iceberg, resulting in the loss of over 1,500 lives. In 1865, President Abraham Lincoln was assassinated, marking a heartbreaking end to his leadership during the post-Civil War period. In 1947, Jackie Robinson broke the color barrier in Major League Baseball, a pivotal moment in the Civil Rights Movement in the United States.

Born on April 15th, you're a natural leader with a fearless spirit and a deep sense of purpose. Your ambition and intelligence make you a pioneer, and the influence of the number 1 only enhances your ability to stand out and create new beginnings. The world is ready for your bold, dynamic presence.

Chapter Sixty-Nine

Born on April 16

If you were born on April 16th, you're an Aries, the zodiac's fearless ram. You are a radiant presence, fueled by the dynamic energy of Mars, which gives you a sense of purpose and an unyielding determination to succeed. This planetary influence shapes you into a natural leader—bold, assertive, and relentlessly driven to reach your goals.

Independence is deeply ingrained in you, and you thrive on making a significant impact in whatever you pursue. Your adventurous nature craves new experiences, and you embrace challenges as opportunities for growth, always pushing forward with confidence.

Your personality is magnetic, drawing others in with ease. You have a way with words, expressing your thoughts with passion and conviction that inspires those around you. People find your presence motivating, and you often serve as a source of encouragement for others to follow your lead.

You excel in competitive environments, where your ability to overcome obstacles shines through. These challenges become a stage where you can display your skills and set ambitious goals, fueling your relentless pursuit of excellence.

With a clear vision of your aspirations, you are never afraid to take calculated risks, stepping outside your comfort zone. Your resilience and determination allow you to bounce back from setbacks, always staying focused on your journey forward.

Your mind is sharp, constantly seeking new knowledge and opportunities to grow. Your analytical skills and problem-solving abilities make you exceptionally skilled at finding innovative solutions, allowing you to tackle even the most complex issues with ease.

In relationships, you are passionate and loyal, with honesty and directness forming the foundation of your connections. You seek partners who can match your intensity and drive, and once you commit, you offer unwavering support and protection to those you love.

Though your impulsiveness can be a strength, it's important to cultivate patience and self-control. By taking a moment to reflect before acting, you can ensure your decisions align with your long-term goals.

In your career, you thrive in leadership roles that demand initiative and vision. You excel in positions where you can take decisive action and make a lasting impact. Whether in entrepreneurship, management, sales, or any field that allows you to showcase your abilities, you are driven to succeed.

The number 2 in numerology adds an extra layer to your Aries traits, bringing balance, cooperation, and a desire for harmonious relationships. This influence strengthens your leadership with empathy, enabling you to be assertive while also understanding the needs and feelings of those around you. The number 2 enhances your ability to build bridges, making you a respected and effective leader.

Careers involving collaboration or helping others may also appeal to you. Fields like counseling, teaching, or social work align with your desire to create supportive and nurturing environments. You also have a natural sensitivity to human emotions, making you a trusted confidante and friend.

While Aries is known for being impulsive, the number 2 encourages you to be mindful of the impact your actions have on others. It helps you find compromise and solutions that benefit everyone involved, ensuring that your actions come from a place of understanding and care.

April 16th has its own historical significance. In 1964, the Ford Mustang was unveiled at the New York World's Fair, quickly becoming an icon of American automotive culture. In 2003, the Treaty of Accession was signed in Athens, expanding the European Union by 10 new member states. And in 1972, NASA's Apollo 16 mission to the moon was launched, furthering our understanding of lunar geology.

Born on April 16th, you are a unique blend of assertive leadership and a heart that seeks harmony. Your ability to balance your drive for success with compassion allows you to build meaningful connections and make a positive impact on the world around you. With your empathetic approach, the world is ready for your passionate, dynamic presence.

Chapter Seventy

Born on April 17

Born on April 17th, you are an Aries, the pioneering ram with a natural flair for leadership. Mars, your ruling planet, infuses you with an infectious confidence and enthusiasm. You are driven by determination and an unwavering desire for success, making you someone destined to leave a lasting mark on the world. Boldness and courage define you, and your independence shines brightly. You have a deep desire to make a meaningful impact, and no challenge feels too great to overcome. Every step you take is guided by an unwavering focus on your goals.

Your charisma is undeniable. You have a way of captivating others with your magnetic presence, and your ability to communicate is exceptional. Your words are filled with passion, conviction, and persuasive power, drawing people in and inspiring them to take action. You naturally motivate those around you, creating a sense of excitement and energy wherever you go. In competitive environments, you thrive. You excel in overcoming obstacles, using them as opportunities to prove your abilities. Setting ambitious goals fuels your determination, and you never shy away from a challenge.

Your vision is clear, and you are not afraid to take calculated risks to achieve your dreams. Resilience is your strength, and even in the face of setbacks, you remain laser-focused on your journey. This fearless attitude propels you forward, no matter the difficulty. In relationships, you are passionate and loyal. Honesty and directness are your guiding principles, and you seek partners who can match your intensity and dedication. You are fiercely protective of those you love, always offering unwavering support.

While impulsiveness can be one of your strengths, it's important for you to nurture patience and self-control. These qualities help ensure that your actions align with your long-term vision and goals. In your career, you thrive in leadership roles where initiative and a pioneering spirit are essential. Positions where you can take charge and make decisive choices allow you to shine. Entrepreneurship, management, sales, and other fields that let you display your talents and make a significant impact are ideal for you.

The number 3 in numerology adds an exciting creative dimension to your already dynamic Aries traits. Creativity, self-expression, and a deep love for connection are influenced by the number 3, enhancing your natural leadership with artistic flair. You have a unique ability to inspire others with your vision and communicate your ideas in a way that captivates. This creative spark makes you a compelling leader, motivating others with both your assertiveness and your ability to express yourself.

Your artistic side may find fulfillment in careers that involve music, art, writing, or acting. These creative fields allow you to channel your assertiveness into something truly impactful, helping you stand out in your chosen area. The influence of the number 3 also brings a sense of playfulness and joy to your life. Your positive outlook and sense of humor make you a delightful companion, and your ability to find joy in the everyday adds a refreshing perspective to any situation.

While Aries energy can sometimes be impulsive, the number 3 encourages you to channel your energy into constructive, expressive outlets. Roles in teaching, mentoring, or any profession where you can inspire and uplift others may bring you great satisfaction and fulfillment.

April 17th holds significant historical moments as well. In 1961, the Bay of Pigs invasion took place, a failed attempt by Cuban exiles to overthrow Fidel Castro's regime. In 1970, the Apollo 13 mission safely returned to Earth after a life-threatening explosion, a testament to human resilience and problem-solving. Four years later, on April 17th, 1975, the Khmer Rouge took control of Cambodia, leading to a tragic genocide that lasted until 1979.

As someone born on April 17th, you are a unique blend of assertive leadership and creative energy. Your ability to communicate passionately and effectively makes you a powerful force, inspiring those around you. The world is ready for your vibrant spirit, Aries, and with your creative spark, you're poised to make a lasting impact wherever you go.

Born on April 18

Born on April 18th, you're an Aries, known for your boldness and fearless nature. Confidence and charisma are central to your personality, and your enthusiasm lights up any room you walk into. Driven by Mars, the planet of action, you're determined and always striving for success. Leadership comes naturally to you, and you're constantly seeking opportunities to carve your own path in the world. Your adventurous spirit pushes you to embrace new experiences and tackle challenges head-on, with an unwavering determination to succeed.

You have an innate magnetism that draws people to you, and your communication skills are remarkable. When you speak, your words carry weight, and you can persuade and inspire others with ease. Your infectious optimism motivates those around you, pushing them to pursue their dreams and take action.

Whether you're leading a team or simply offering advice, your passion and energy encourage people to rise to their full potential.

With a relentless desire to achieve, you're always setting ambitious goals. Competitive by nature, you thrive in environments where you can showcase your skills and abilities. Every challenge becomes an opportunity to prove yourself, and you're constantly pushing your own limits to reach greater heights. Your sharp intellect and curiosity fuel your desire for knowledge, making you a lifelong learner. You're always exploring new ideas and expanding your understanding of the world, which makes you a valuable asset in any pursuit. Your innovative thinking and problem-solving abilities allow you to overcome obstacles with ease.

In relationships, you're a loyal and protective partner who values honesty and authenticity. You seek a connection with someone who can match your energy and enthusiasm for life. Your commitment to those you care about is unwavering, and you're always ready to offer support and stand up for them when needed. While you're driven and assertive, you also recognize the importance of balance. Your impulsiveness can sometimes lead to rash decisions, so cultivating patience and self-control is essential to ensure your actions align with your long-term goals.

In your career, you excel in leadership roles where initiative and independence are key. Whether in entrepreneurship, management, or sales, you're suited for positions where you can make decisions and drive results. Your assertiveness and determination are assets in any field that requires a proactive approach and a results-oriented mindset.

Numerology also plays a role in shaping your character. The number 4 brings a sense of stability, organization, and a methodical approach to your Aries traits. While your natural drive is focused on achieving goals, the influence of number 4 helps you stay grounded and disciplined. You have a practical, structured approach to leadership, balancing your assertiveness with a focus on building lasting success. Your attention to detail and your ability to plan strategically make you well-suited for roles that require problem-solving and long-term thinking. The number 4 also enhances your reliability, making you someone others can count on, particularly in challenging situations. By channeling your energy into thoughtful and strategic actions, you'll find fulfillment and success in any endeavor.

Looking at history, on April 18th, significant events have unfolded. In 1906, the Great San Francisco Earthquake struck, causing widespread devastation and changing the city's infrastructure forever. In 1980, Zimbabwe gained independence from British colonial rule, marking a new era for the nation. Also, in 1946, the International Court of Justice held its inaugural session, laying the foundation for the future of international law and justice.

If you're born on April 18th, you're a remarkable blend of bold leadership and practical thinking. Your ability to combine enthusiasm with strategic focus allows you to achieve great things and inspire those around you. The world is waiting for your drive and vision, and with the added influence of number 4, you're poised to make your mark in meaningful ways.

Born on April 19

Born on April 19th, you are an Aries, the fearless ram of the zodiac. Your personality is dynamic, radiating confidence, enthusiasm, and a unique spark. Fueled by Mars, the planet of action, you embody determination, leadership, and an unwavering drive to excel.

Taking charge comes naturally to you. An independent spirit fuels your desire to make a lasting impact on whatever you pursue, and your adventurous soul thrives on new experiences. Challenges are nothing more than stepping stones on your path to success. You are a captivating communicator, drawing others in with your charm and passion. Your ability to express ideas with conviction and inspire others to take action makes you a natural leader.

In competitive environments, you thrive. These arenas become your proving ground, where you showcase your skills and determination. You set ambitious goals, and your relentless pursuit of excellence fuels your drive to achieve them. Your vision is clear, and you are unafraid to take calculated risks to push beyond your comfort zone. With determination and resilience as your armor, you bounce back from setbacks and stay laser-focused on your journey.

Curiosity is a constant companion in your life. With a sharp intellect and a thirst for knowledge, you seek to expand your understanding and explore new ideas. Your problem-solving skills and analytical mind make you an invaluable asset in any endeavor. In love, you are a loyal partner who values honesty and genuineness. You seek someone who can match your energy and zest for life, offering unwavering support and protection to those you care about.

While your independent streak is a strength, it can sometimes lead to stubbornness. Being open to different perspectives and working with others can enhance your journey. You thrive in leadership roles that demand initiative and a pioneering spirit. Whether in entrepreneurship, management, or sales, your natural drive to take charge makes you well-suited for fields that require assertiveness and results-driven action.

The number 5 in numerology influences your journey, representing freedom, creativity, and a desire for progress. This influence strengthens your leadership and adds a focus on initiative and adaptability. You excel at planning, decision-making, and navigating challenges with confidence. When focused on a goal, you devote your full energy to achieving it, creating opportunities for yourself and others. Self-reliance is important to you, and your resilience empowers you to overcome obstacles and build your path to success.

Your love for learning and creative thinking allows you to generate innovative ideas. As a partner, you shine by sharing your dreams and supporting those you care about, always ready to offer a shoulder to lean on. While your independence is important, listening to others and being open to different perspectives will strengthen your relationships.

On this day in history, significant events have occurred that reflect the same spirit of resilience and change you embody. On April 19, 1956, the Revolución Libertadora in Argentina led to the overthrow of the government, marking a political shift. In 1943, the Warsaw Ghetto Uprising began, symbolizing Jewish resistance against Nazi oppression. And in 1961, Sierra Leone gained independence from British rule, marking the end of colonial control.

Being born on April 19th means you're not just a superstar, but a leader with a drive for progress and education. Your ability to blend initiative with a thirst for knowledge allows you to achieve great things. The world is ready for your bold and dynamic energy, Aries!

Robert J Dornan Books

All Robert J Dornan books can be found on every major platform and in thousands of libraries. Many are also available in French, Spanish, German, and Tagalog. Available in e-books, paperback, and Audio

Fiction:

23 Minutes Past 1 A.M. (Bestseller)

Gwydion

Lost in Jack City (Coming Soon)

Non-Fiction

Lucky You: The Ultimate Book of Fortune and 100 Spells

Everything You Need to Know About the Chinese Sign, Ox

Everything You Need to Know About the Chinese Sign, Tiger

Everything You Need to Know About the Chinese Sign, Rabbit

Everything You Need to Know About the Chinese Sign, Dragon

Everything You Need to Know About the Chinese Sign, Snake

Everything You Need to Know About the Chinese Sign, Horse

Everything You Need to Know About the Chinese Sign, Goat

Everything You Need to Know About the Chinese Sign, Monkey

Everything You Need to Know About the Chinese Sign, Rooster

Everything You Need to Know About the Chinese Sign, Dog

Everything You Need to Know About the Chinese Sign, Pig

100 True and Terrifying Ghost Stories

The Great Big Book of Ghosts

50 of History's Most Sinister Demons - Part One

50 Stories and Legends About Vampires

50 Famous Exorcisms

Hexed and Hallowed: The True Story of Witches, Then and Now

Whispers from the Past: 50 Astonishing Reincarnation Stories

Blood and Shadows: Canada's Darkest Crimes and Tragedies

Blood and Shadows: England's Darkest Crimes and Tragedies

Blood and Shadows: Scotland's Darkest Crimes and Tragedies

Blood and Shadows: Ireland's Darkest Crimes and Tragedies

Blood and Shadows: France's Darkest Crimes and Tragedies

Hell 101: A Journey Through Hell Across Time and Culture

For more information, visit https://philippineone.com/shop or

https://robertjdornanbooks.blogspot.com/